WHAT OTHERS ARE SAYING

"I don't know if I've ever met anybody who is more persistently, continuously upbeat and enthusiastic than Mike Turpen, especially when he's helping others. He's a very good man and his life story is a very good read."

— President Bill Clinton

MICHAEL C. TURPEN

Attorney
mturpen@riggsabney.com

528 NW 12th Street   Oklahoma City, OK 73103   (405) 843-9909
riggsabney.com

TURPEN TIME

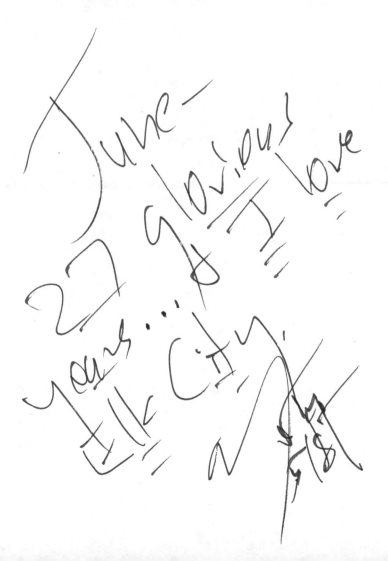

June —
27 glorious
years... I love
Elk City,

TURPEN TIME

THE WIT AND WISDOM OF MIKE TURPEN

MIKE TURPEN

TATE PUBLISHING
AND ENTERPRISES, LLC

Published by Tate Publishing & Enterprises, LLC
127 E. Trade Center Terrace | Mustang, Oklahoma 73064 USA
1.888.361.9473 | www.tatepublishing.com

Tate Publishing is committed to excellence in the publishing industry. The company reflects the philosophy established by the founders, based on Psalm 68:11,
"The Lord gave the word and great was the company of those who published it."

Book design copyright © 2014 by Tate Publishing, LLC. All rights reserved.
Cover design by Ronnel Luspoc
Interior design by Jomel Pepito

Published in the United States of America

ISBN: 978-1-62746-785-8
1. Biography & Autobiography / Personal Memoirs
2. Self-Help / Personal Growth / Happiness
14.04.16

DEDICATION

For my mom, Marge.

And a debt of gratitude to my memorable mentor, Bob Abrams, the Maestro of Manhattan, at least as far as I'm concerned. He introduced me to my literary agent Karen Gantz Zahler, who I met for the first time at the incredible and inimitable Clinton Global Initiative in New York. Karen was a godsend, referring me to Dr Joyce Starr (aka the Book Doctor), who added her unique and special touch to every chapter. I also want to thank the one and only Sheila Williams, who for many years has helped keep me organized and somewhat on schedule. Finally, my profound thanks to all of my friends and supporters—who comprise the stories of my life— for their friendship, knowledge, and wisdom.

CONTENTS

PREFACE

You can't learn to swim by taking a correspond-
ence course.

Call them what you will—epigrams, adages, maxims,
proverbs, aphorisms, truisms, one-liners, or simply
sayings—I love 'em. Like good poetry, the best pack
a ton of revelation and meaning into deceptively
few words.

Take for instance Socrates's famous dictum about
how the unexamined life is not worth living. In a
fundamental way, his wisdom started me on the path
toward writing this book. In examining my own life
to this point—separating the ever-fleeting from the
everlasting—I've concluded that it's our responsibility
to make the best use possible of the life and creativity
that God has bestowed. It's imperative to discover one's
unique voice and gifts. If you can minimize injustice
and intolerance while maximizing respect and kindness,
you will have done your part to make our own corners
of the world better places to live. It's your choice.

Every one of us can add to or subtract from the happiness, peace of mind, and quality of life belonging to those we encounter on our journey, whether we encounter them for only one fleeting moment in our lives or live with them daily.

I often think about sayings I've written down over the years, from "The more you give, the more you have" to remembering that life is generally all about the four Fs—faith, family, friends, and finances. You'll find that four Fs line elsewhere in this book. It's one of fifty chapter-topping maxims I've collected or created over the years, pithy sayings that introduce stories and lessons from my own life.

Another one of my favorites is "Make a living and make a difference." It strikes a chord in a lot of people because few were born into a situation where money, success, and/or fame was/is a gift. Most work and make a living for themselves—and no matter what it is we're doing, we can seize the opportunities to make a lot of difference along the way.

We all have unique life experiences, and most have held many jobs. At various stages of my life, I've been a *Tulsa World* paperboy, a Colgate-Palmolive soap salesman, a Sears Santa Claus, a Steak & Ale waiter, and a McKissick Products forklift operator. I've also been a Muskogee Police Department legal advisor, a Muskogee County district attorney, attorney general of Oklahoma, and a Democratic candidate for governor of Oklahoma. I am now a practicing lawyer, a television commentator, and a fundraiser for worthy causes, among other things.

Through both work and family, I've lived—and learned how to live—an extraordinary life. In our daily struggle for significance, it's imperative to realize that we are not perfect. A few mistakes are better than perfect inaction. Stories you'll read here have humbled me. I share them knowing that we have all been humbled, chastened, and even embarrassed by our actions at various points in our lives. Often, such experiences teach us the best lessons.

We all have our triumphs and joys, and you'll find some of those here as well. They too can teach us. But then we get back to the axiom atop this introduction. It reminds us that we can learn via the OPE method—other people's experiences—but that only goes so far.

People can tell you about different swimmer's strokes and what to do when you get in water over your head, but ultimately, we all have to take the plunge ourselves. I did. We all do.

In the final analysis, then, this is simply a book about being human and learning and trying to do the best that you can—about one man who dove into life many years ago and keeps right on swimming, often-time against the current. I hope my little slice of OPE will entertain, encourage and help you as you travel down your own path. Taking Socrates's words to heart, I've examined my life, coming up with half a hundred stories that run the gamut from amusing to sobering. I hope you enjoy them.

—Mike Turpen
Oklahoma City

"Puff the Magic Dragon" performing in the Tulsa Figure Skating Club Ice Travaganza in 1962. My dad was the head, Brent was the middle and I was the tail. It was a real show stopper.

SHEEP AND GOATS

> You might as well be hanged for a sheep as for
> a goat.

You have just so much God-given energy, and every morning when you get up, the way you use it is your choice. Over the years, I've sought out and read the musings of many of history's great philosophers, and they've all enriched my life. But to this good day, my favorite philosopher is my mother, Marge. I suspect she's the reason I have such an affinity for truisms and inspirational sayings. After all, I began hearing them from her as early in my life as I can remember.

Although my mother is the most well-read person I know, her college was the college of experience. I like to say that she had a variety of graduate degrees from that institution, where the lessons are bumps and bruises and the school colors are black and blue. During my youth, she worked at a rock crusher, dispatching eighteen-wheeler dump trucks all over the area. (At the time, she was affectionately known as the Mother Trucker). That job earned her a steady paycheck that went a long way toward feeding and clothing my two brothers and me. It was hard work, not ivory-tower stuff. But regardless of how she made her living, she was, and is, the smartest person I've ever known.

Plus, she has never had a negative thought nor a negative day in her whole life. She's beaten heart trouble and cancer, again and again, and she's never complained one minute. She came from a Depression-era family in Hamilton, Missouri, her dad a law officer killed in the line of duty, and I know it must have been tough for her while she was growing up. But she was not one of those older folks who talked about their health or how hard the times used to be or any of that sort of downer conversation.

I know it must have been hard for her too when Dad would get down and depressed. But my mother's always been up and away. She was an inspiration—the ultimate life enhancer.

Her screen door swung open on welcome hinges. The kids I grew up with, our neighborhood bunch, were forever coming in and out of our house. She treated the youngsters in the neighborhood like she treated her own, and they responded by loving her and wanting to be around her just as we did. Our yard wasn't the most beautiful one in the neighborhood, simply because a steady stream of kids always seemed to be running through it. Someone once asked her, "Can't you grow grass on your yard?"

Her response: "I'm not growing grass. I'm growing boys."

Above her hearth, there was a brass plaque that read, "The ornament of a house is the friends that frequent it." That tells you a lot about my mother and what was important to her. She was a friend to everyone she met. Like our great native son, Will Rogers, my mom never met a person she didn't like.

Her welcoming nature was embodied in her philosophy of life: every morning, when you get up, you have only a certain amount of God-given energy. You can use it positively or negatively. It's up to you. And her suggestion to her three sons was always, "For God's sake, use it in a positive way."

I remember, when I was in the seventh grade, I came home one day and told her that I'd decided to run for class treasurer.

"Why not president?" she asked.

I explained that the most popular kid in class was running for president, and I was afraid I might get beat.

"You might as well be hanged for a sheep as for a goat," she returned.

Now I'm not sure that my seventh grade mind could quite wrap all the way around that ancient bit of wisdom, but I think I got what I needed. And just in case I didn't, she had other axioms to spring on me, like "If you shoot at the moon and miss, you'll still land among the stars." She also told me her thoughts on risk and reward and how the potential reward grows with the potential risk involved.

"Mike," she'd say, "if you have a rope on the floor and you walk on it like you would a tightrope, there's not much risk there—and not much reward. But if you take that rope and fix it where it's six feet off the floor—well, that's another story."

I ran for class president instead of treasurer, and I won. From there, I eventually won the race for Muskogee County district attorney and then Oklahoma attorney general. She helped in every race by commandeering a dump truck, filling it with Turpen supporters, and roaring off to every parade and festival in Oklahoma. My brother Frosty even met his wife-to-be, Gayla, during the Turpen truck's appearance at the 1982 Huckleberry Festival in Jay. That truck, and my mom's ingenuity in putting it to creative use, had a big impact on both of our lives.

Looking back, I can see that a lot of my mother's sayings point toward the same conclusion: take chances. Don't be afraid. Use your God-given energy in positive ways. I remember a sampler she gave me once that read, "A ship in a harbor is safe, but that's not what ships are built for." That was her philosophy. You've got to sail on. Lift your sails; capture the winds of your destiny. She also liked to say that if you catch on fire with enthusiasm, people will come from miles around just to watch you burn.

So much of what she said over the years, coupled with the way she lived, continues to have a profound effect on my life. If not for her words, I might have missed many of the risks I've taken in my life, all leading, with the grace of God, to successful careers in politics, law, and public speaking.

I'm not sure if it came from her—although I expect that it did—but there's another truism that applies to my mother: You can accomplish anything if you don't mind who gets the credit.

When my dad and my brothers performed in the *Puff, the Magic Dragon* sketch for the Tulsa Figure Skating Club's Ice Travaganza, who do you think made the elaborate multiperson dragon costume? Sure, it was Marge. She put a bunch of hula hoops together, covered them with material, sewed the material, built the whole thing—and then my dad and my brothers got all the glory. People were enthusiastic after our performance, coming up and telling us, "Boy, what a great dragon." At the same time, Mom was saying privately, "That *damn* dragon."

That's how she always referred to it. She took her time and effort and creativity to build it so we could go out there and take our turns in the spotlight. She labored for hours transforming scraps of cloth and hula hoops into a work of pop art, something the rest of her family could admire and wow the crowd with it. (The word *mom* upside down, as I've often said, is *wow*.) But that's the way of Marge: always putting the kids—and grandkids—out there, while she stayed in the background. She just wanted all of us to be the best we could be. Credit wasn't important to her.

That doesn't mean she wasn't flattered when she received attention. After we helped Hillary Clinton carry the state in the 2008 presidential primary, Bill Clinton called out of the blue one day and said, "Mike, is there anything I can do for you?"

I said, "I'll tell you what, Mr. President, there is. My mother is eighty years old today. Would you be able to call her and wish her a happy birthday?"

Two hours later, my mother called from Wagoner, up on Lake Fort Gibson, and the first thing I heard when I pick up the receiver was, "You're not going to believe what happened! Bill Clinton just called and wished me a happy birthday!"

That was one of the best moments of my life.

In a letter to the graduating class at Colorado's Naropa University, Alice Walker, author of *The Color Purple*, wrote, "One thing I have learned is that just as we are lucky enough to live on a planet that has mornings, there is such a thing as a human sunrise." She exhorted the graduates to seek out human sunrises and to stay close to them once they were found.

I don't have to look very far to find my own.

Marge Turpen Shahan is a human sunrise, a force that transforms our imperfect world into a better place. She was a human sunrise when she was raising my brothers and me—advising us, helping us into adulthood, holding the family together, working hard, fighting health issues, but never having a bad day. She continues to be one of those rare human sunrises, a great, unflagging force for good to all who know her.

My mom always wanted me to put pen to paper. And despite being more of a talker than a writer—something she knows very well—I've now sailed out of the harbor, attached the tightrope six feet high instead of leaving it on the floor, shot at the moon, gone after a sheep instead of a goat, and written a book.

For her sake, I hope I've gotten it right.

MAKE IT COUNT

Earn it.

Adages that lead off the chapters in this book can be applied to a variety of situations. But none are more relevant than "Make it count." What does it mean, exactly? Make *what* count? Perhaps it's everything you learn in life. Maybe it's life itself. Or perhaps it's someone else's life.

The hardest public speaking I've ever done was on November 26, 2006. Five days before that date—one day before Thanksgiving—young Harrison Neal, the son of my law partner Gary Neal, was found dead in his bedroom. He'd been taking cold medicine, and the family believed that he'd accidentally overdosed when he added OxyContin, the prescription painkiller that made headlines a couple of years ago when controversial conservative commentator Rush Limbaugh was arrested for obtaining it illegally.

November 26 was the date of Harrison's service. His parents had asked me to do the eulogy. They'd told me that there would be probably two hundred of Harrison's classmates from Tulsa's Booker T. Washington High School there, and "You're going to save at least one of those kids' lives with what you say."

There's no way of knowing if we saved any lives that day, but we did our best, and I did what the parents asked me to do. In the eulogy, I talked about the question that our great American poet Robert Frost was asked on his eightieth birthday. Someone had said, "Mr. Frost, what's the most important thing you learned in your eighty years?"

He'd replied with only three words, "Life goes on."

That's how I started my eulogy. And with those two hundred Booker T. kids all down front in the midst of a standing-room-only crowd, I continued by talking about the pain and struggle of trying to get your children across the river, that treacherous river of abuse, and onto the shore of recovery. I talked about how all the love and respect in the world may still not be enough to get your child across that river.

When they have problems with their children, most parents are reluctant to go outside the family for solutions. I'm sure that's a universal feeling, but it seems to be especially prevalent in this part of the country, with its self-sufficient pioneer spirit and a legacy of facing and triumphing over all kinds of physical and spiritual adversity. In a lot of Oklahoma families, going to a counselor for help might even be interpreted as nothing more than a sign of weakness.

I'm here, as an old north Tulsa boy, to tell you that's not right. Someone might come to me, in confidence, and say, "Well, we're having trouble with our son. It may be drugs. It may be alcohol. We don't know what to do about it."

And I'll say, "What do you do for a living?"

"I'm an electrician."

"That's right," I'll say. "You're a very good one too. I'm a lawyer, and I'm pretty good. But I'm not a counselor. You're not a counselor either. They can't do what we do, but we can't do what *they* do, either. So go see a family counselor. They're good at what they do."

I've never been sanctimonious or evangelical about counseling, but because I've gone through it myself, personally, I feel that I know enough about it to recommend it to others.

It was counseling, in fact, that led me to a deeper understanding of the maxim: "The definition of insanity is doing the same thing over and over again and expecting different results." In a general sense, it could apply to any parent who knows there's a problem with a child, but goes along as if nothing has changed and simply hopes that things will get better.

I've also seen a specific illustration of that wisdom. In fact, you could say that I acted it out when a counselor walked over to where I was sitting. "What's your name?" he asked.

"Mike. Mike Turpen."

"All right, Mike." He gestured toward a closed door, across the room. "I want you to get up and knock that door down."

This was in front of the whole group, and I wasn't sure what was going on. *Maybe he picked me because of my size*, I thought. I was the biggest guy in the room, and if anyone there could take the door down, I was the best bet to do it. In a courtroom, I knew what I was doing and what to expect. Counseling was his area of expertise, not mine.

"You want me to do what?" I asked.

"I want you to knock that door down."

"Right now?"

"Right now," he said.

I reminded myself that I was in his world, so I was going to do exactly what he told me to do. I took a run at the door, hit it hard—and it didn't budge.

"What do you think?" he asked.

I said, "What do you *mean* what do I think?"

"I asked you to knock the door down," he responded.

I backed up and charged the door like a football lineman, putting my shoulder into it. *Wham!* The collision jarred me all over, but the door didn't move.

"Well," the counselor said, "you're not going to knock that door down, are you?"

"I don't know," I returned. "I can try again. But maybe I won't."

"Go ahead. Try again."

This time, I *really* tried to take that door off its hinges. I slammed into it with all the force I could muster, giving it everything I had, and truth to tell, it did budge a little. But not much.

"Okay," he said, "sit down, Mike."

When I was seated, he looked us all over for a moment. Finally, he said, "You have just seen the definition of insanity—doing the same thing over and over again and expecting different results. To think you're going to do the same thing over and over with these kids and expect a different result to come out of it—that's *insanity!* The reason you're here is so that you can change what you've been doing and get a different result. You have to do something *different.*"

I have been lucky and blessed to help others make it across that treacherous river.

But some good kids, for reasons that defy any glib explanations, sink beneath the waters, lost to us forever. It could happen to anyone's child. It did happen to Harrison. His death was a tragedy almost beyond endurance for his parents, as it would've been for any of us.

Through their pain and their grief, Gary and his family were determined to make his life count. As I stood before that solemn crowd at Harrison's funeral, I was too.

"Today," I said, "I choose not to add Harrison's name to that long list of young people taken by senseless tragedies of life and just be done with it. Let's not pray for his soul and then be done with it. Let's not comfort his family and be done with it. Let's not say 'Time heals all wounds' and 'This too shall pass' and be done with it. I say we choose to be proactive and redemptive."

And then I called up an image from *Saving Private Ryan,* the blockbuster war movie from 1998. In it, Tom Hanks's character, Captain Miller, is dying in the arms of Matt Damon's character, Private Ryan, and Captain Miller says, "Earn it. *Earn* it."

Locking eyes with some of those kids from Booker T., I echoed that two-word phrase. Then I said, "To me, that means 'Make it count.' When the captain says, 'Earn it,' what he's really telling the private is 'Make my life count. Make *your* life count.'"

Pausing to let the idea sink in, I added, "I'm saying make your life count and make Harrison Lucas Neal's life count by remembering how he lived and how he died. You can learn from that."

Those kids went back to their high school, and soon many of them had started wearing bracelets with the inscription, Make It Count.

Did Harrison's death save any lives? Did it count? I think it did, and it's still counting. Gary, his father, has become involved with the Partnership for Drug Free America and Palmer Continuum of Care, a drug-treatment center for women and teenagers, and he speaks often about his son. In his determination for Harrison's death not to have been in vain, Gary has become a highly visible force against drug addiction.

In an article in the *Tulsa World* on September 27, 2007, Barbara Allen wrote, "Gary thinks that maybe if he talks openly about Harrison, supports a run [the Palmer Walk/Run for a Drug Free Life], donates some money, becomes a media poster child for drug abuse's heartache. . .well, that will help somebody else. Someone he probably doesn't know. Like all parents who've lost a child, he said, 'I wouldn't wish this pain on my own worst enemy.'"

Because fellow students wore bracelets inscribed with his name virtually everywhere, and given his own father's willingness to talk about the personal toll of teenage drug abuse, Harrison Neal's life continues to count. His friends and family have made it count as they've touched lives and helped others all in the name of a bright and sensitive young man who, sadly, was not able to make it across that dark, lonely river but who still shines on in the hearts and souls of all who knew him.

Turpen Poetry Club--2009--Front L to R: Turner Peterson, Ford Price, David Price, Johnny Vater, Patrick Turpen. Back: Ryan Randolph and Niki Bray.

TAKE IT PERSONALLY

If you don't take it personally, don't take it at all.

Elsewhere in this book is a chapter on my great mentor Mr. E. M. Guillory, who I met when I was a young Muskogee County assistant district attorney. He was serving in the DA's office when I got there, and I quickly became his student and protégé.

Guillory was a wise man, and he taught me a lot. He taught me, for instance, that I have to take a law-enforcement job like ours personally in order to do it right. I'm sure he'd seen many people get hardened and cynical and detached in the course of facing a relentless parade of crime and criminals day after day. He'd seen people insulate themselves emotionally against the sadness and horror that the victims felt too, and while I'm sure he knew that distancing yourself was a kind of survival mechanism, he told me over and over the axiom that heads this chapter: "If you don't take it personally, don't take it at all."

Of course, when you're a DA taking your cases personally, it's easy to get angry and frustrated when the gears of justice don't grind quickly—or fairly—enough. The perception that the system is biased in favor of the criminal is a hard one to shake. As a district attorney, I always tried to remember those powerful lines from Sir Thomas More (played by Paul Scofield) in the movie *A Man for All Seasons*, when a courtroom opponent incredulously states that More would "give the devil the benefit of law."

More responds that he would indeed, unlike his accuser. Otherwise, he says, "When the last law was down, and the devil turned round on you, where would you hide, Roper, the laws all being flat? This country is planted thick with laws, from coast to coast, man's laws, not God's! And if you cut them down, and you're just the man to do it, do you really think you could stand upright in the winds that would blow then? Yes, I'd give the devil benefit of law for my own safety's sake!"

He was saying that you had to guarantee even Satan himself the presumption of innocence under the law. I had to think hard about that idea during our successful prosecution of Charles Troy Coleman—written about more fully in another chapter—who cold-bloodedly murdered John and Roxie Seward after they'd arrived at John's sister's house in rural Muskogee to find Coleman burglarizing it. It was a particularly evil crime, with Coleman taking them to the basement and coldly blasting their lives away with a shotgun. The weapon, as it turned out, was unusual: a .28 gauge pump shotgun.

We later found federal brand .28 gauge shells on Coleman's bedside table, just one more piece of evidence in what we saw as an overwhelming case against him. When he was caught, he had the Sewards' wallets with him, their driver's licenses, and even beef from their freezer! We ran a picture of his pickup in the newspaper, asking if anyone had seen it at the Seward's home around the time of the killings, and sure enough, a couple came forward and said, "Yeah, we drove by their house and saw the truck there." With very substantial help from the Oklahoma State Bureau of Investigation, we quickly put a strong case together.

But Coleman, unsurprisingly, denied everything. He was a glib guy, a longtime con man with ten or fifteen previous convictions who'd become an accomplished liar. So when we caught him with property from the house, including the wallets, he told us that he'd picked up some strangers who'd left that stuff in the back of his pickup, and gosh, they must have left those wallets too. We had so much on him, and he knew it, but he continued to deny everything.

After we'd interviewed him Friday and gotten nowhere, I went home for a couple of days to Owasso, where my mother was then living. But all weekend long, I brooded over Coleman and what he'd done to those people, thinking about how he was blithely lying about it all. It preyed on me. He was caught, and he simply refused to admit it.

I kept tossing it over and over in my mind, and then Monday morning I made my decision. I was going to go face-to-face with Coleman, one on one.

Almost before I knew it, I was in Muskogee, at the county jail, being let into Coleman's cell. I'd left Owasso around 7:00 a.m. An hour later, I was poking my finger in Coleman's face.

"Charles," I said, "you told me Friday night that you picked up a couple of strangers. That's not going to work. We've found the Sewards' property at your home. We've found the kind of ammunition the Sewards were killed with on your bedside table. Charles. Charles. It's not going to work." I kept waving my finger at him, and I know my voice rose out of frustration and emotion. "We're going to put you right down there in the basement where you shot those two people," I said. "I'm going to put you down there with my evidence. I'm going to put you *right down there!*"

"You can't!" he shouted. "You can't prove it!" Even as he spoke, he was backing away from me.

I kept pressing. "I'm going to put you *down there* in the *basement*—where you were when you killed John and Roxie Seward! I'm putting you *down* there!"

At that point, Gary Sturm—my investigator from the DA's office—showed up and took me by the arm. I'd called him that morning, telling him I was going to the jail. I guess I'd almost worked myself into some kind of trance because all I remember now is him saying, "Mike, Mike, listen to me," then to Coleman, "Charles, we'll talk to you later, buddy." I recall Sturm leading me out of the cell and away from the jail.

Looking back, I'm frankly not sure if what I did that morning was completely legal. I didn't lay a hand on him but pressed for a confession (which we never obtained).

At times, I still wonder what I was thinking. Charles Troy Coleman was a coldblooded murderer, a hardened criminal perfectly willing to murder someone. I was a young Dudley Do-Right DA on a crusade—Buford Pusser in *Walking Tall*. With no wife or family, I was bulletproof. Angry and frustrated, it was important to go man-to-man. I took those murders personally.

Did my diatribe do any good? I don't know. What I do know is that we made our case step by step; Coleman was put on death row, and he ultimately became the first Oklahoma inmate to die by lethal injection.

Throughout my days in the Muskogee district attorney's office and during my time as state attorney general, seeing justice done remained a very personal thing to me. Although I'm in private practice now, not a DA or AG, I'd still guarantee the devil the presumption of innocence, but I'd make it my personal business to go toe-to-toe with him until justice was done.

Poetry Club members and fathers on the Salmon River in Idaho on a 100-mile rafting trip in 2010. A passage from Hemingway's "For Whom the Bell Tolls" captured the essence of this magnificent journey:

I had an inheritance from my father,
It was the moon and the sun,
And though I roam all over the world,
The spending of it's never done.

JUNIOR HIGH FOREVER

You're only young once, but you have the potential to be immature forever.

When the famed NBC-TV newsman Tom Brokaw gave the commencement address at Skidmore College, he told the graduating class and assembled guests, "You've been told during your high school years and your college years that you are now about to enter the real world, and you've been wondering what it's like. Let me tell you that the real world is not college.

"The real world is not high school. The real world, it turns out, is much more like junior high. You are going to encounter, for the rest of your life, the same petty jealousies, the same irrational juvenile behavior, the same uncertainty that you encountered during your adolescent years. That is your burden. We all share it with you. We wish you well."

As Brokaw noted, we may be young only once, but there's no age limit on irrational, inappropriate, or adolescent behavior. People can strike out like angry kids no matter what age they are. Take the following experience for instance.

Back when I was Muskogee County district attorney, I had the responsibility of condemning a rural road in order to put through a school-bus route. There was some controversy attached to the case because it involved taking some land from a local farmer and rancher. His name was J. D. Masterson. He was seventy-five years old, and he wasn't happy about what we were doing. Applying the philosophy of "delegate or stagnate," I asked Assistant DA Tom Alford to handle the case. He did, but Mr. Masterson still held me accountable for the attempt to take his land for the greater good.

One day, I was walking out of the Muskogee County Courthouse on the way to lunch, blissfully unaware that the hearing for condemning the road had just concluded and Mr. Masterson had lost. Suddenly there he was right in front of me, snarling, "Why, you—" and swinging at me. I managed to duck just as he swung, but his fist still slammed soundly against the side of my head.

I kept my feet. But not my dignity.

"Arrest that man!" I yelled as the pugnacious septuagenarian fled down the courthouse steps. "Arrest that man!"

However, even though a deputy gave chase, Masterson eluded the law and disappeared from the streets of Muskogee.

Eventually, he came back to town and gave himself up, pleading guilty to assault on a public official and paying the one-hundred-dollar fine without complaint.

I have no doubt that he figured it was worth the money. Like the kid on the playground who decks someone he thinks needs it and then proudly faces up to the principal's punishment, Mr. Masterson probably considered his fine as a badge of honor.

The next day, the headline in the *Muskogee Phoenix* newspaper shouted, "Pay 100 Bucks and Punch the DA." It sounded like a new game for the upcoming Muskogee State Fair. Fortunately, though, there were no other takers.

The idea of a septuagenarian settling the score like a jacked-up junior-high football player put me in mind of the axiom about how all of us adults have the potential to be immature to the end of our days. And truth to tell, after taking the blow, I should have been a little more mature about my response as well. But JD's punch brought something else home to me. It made me realize that I had to be man enough to handle the hot, controversial cases myself—man to man, if you will—and not pass them off to someone else. As Give-'em-Hell-Harry famously said, "If you can't stand the heat, get out of the kitchen."

Our thirty-third president made his comment when he was at the top, the leader of the greatest country in the world. But as my run-in with J. D. Masterson showed me, Truman's observation could apply to situations at any level, including, surely, to the Muskogee County district attorney.

Being named Muskogee County District Attorney by Oklahoma's 21st governor, David Boren, 1977.

CHANGE THE GAME

Personal contact alters opinions.

You'll find me going back to the case of Charles Troy Coleman several times in this book. I have many reasons for doing so. Perhaps the biggest one is that I believed then, and still do, that it was a simple case of good versus evil. As a district attorney, I often saw shades of gray. But with Coleman, I did not.

I was convinced that he was a coldblooded killer who would kill again and again if given the chance. He was like a pie with a piece missing—unsalvageable in any way, except by a power far higher than mine. My job was for the jury to believe in his irredeemable character to have the requisite fear, outrage, and courage necessary not just to find him guilty but to recommend the death penalty.

As I was pressing forward toward that goal though, a strange thing happened.

You've heard the old saw about how familiarity breeds contempt? Sometimes, it's just the opposite.

Sometimes, even a murderer who's committed repeated monstrous crimes almost becomes, to some of those around him, just another guy.

In 1979, when I was prosecuting Coleman for the horrific murders of John and Roxie Seward, I came into the courtroom with a changed appearance. I'd been sporting a moustache, but after the case was moved to Cherokee County, I decided it might be prudent to look a little more clean-cut than I had in Muskogee County, where I was DA, so I shaved it off.

Coleman started needling me. "Oh, you shaved your moustache," he said. "You shaved it just for me, didn't you? You're getting all cleaned up, aren't you?" He knew that my purpose was to send him to death row; yet he was teasing me as though we were both kids on the playground—as if he wasn't a hardened killer. For a moment, he seemed human.

A lot of people beside me had spent time with Coleman during his trial, and some of them were almost close to him—because, again, personal contact alters opinions.

There's also a very real inclination, subconscious though it may be, to appease, placate, and pacify someone who might do you harm. A variation of this is the Stockholm Syndrome, named after an incident in Stockholm, Sweden, in which a group took a number of bank employees hostage. Almost a week later, when a rescue was made, some of the hostages resisted their rescuers, siding instead with their captors—whom they had come to see, through personal contact, as not only fellow humans, but as people with the ability to hurt them if the relationship turned unfriendly.

An example closer to the Coleman case came when writer Truman Capote launched a new kind of novelistic non-fiction with his 1965 novel *In Cold Blood*. The story of the grisly murder of a family by two psychopathic drifters, it required extensive interviews with the murderers, and Capote himself admitted that his relationship with the two became almost like friendship.

That's akin to how some of the people in Coleman's orbit began feeling. I remember coming into court once when the jury was in the box, and one of the deputies was handing Coleman a cup of coffee, making small talk, the way you might do with a friend. I had to call him aside and say, "Whoa. This is a man who *murdered* three people, and you're treating him like a regular human being in front of the jury. No. You can't do that."

You have to control every perception that the jury has, even during a break. And if a deputy or some other law-enforcement agent is lighting a murderer's cigarette or bringing him a cup of coffee, it subliminally creates the perception that the person on trial is just plain folks, a decent guy who deserves decent treatment.

In Coleman's case though, here was a man who'd emptied a shotgun into two people, slit the throat of an Oklahoma officer and left him to die, killed another man in Tulsa, and then taken another officer hostage before finally being captured in an Arizona manhunt.

In short, Charles Troy Coleman wasn't exactly the kind of guy you'd want for a next-door neighbor, and regardless of how personal contact with him had altered the perceptions of some who were entrusted with his care, I had to make sure that the members of the jury understood just what kind of a person they had before them.

They must have understood because they gave him the death penalty.

UNFORGETTABLE CHARACTERS

> You'll win more cases in the law library than
> you ever will in the courtroom.
>
> —Pat Williams

If you're of baby-boomer age or older, you'll probably remember a recurring feature that ran for years in *Reader's Digest*. It was called "My Most Unforgettable Character," and it featured first-person stories from people about the often-colorful figures who'd made a lasting impression on their lives.

For me, that unforgettable character was Patrick A. Williams.

Pat was a real-life Atticus Finch, the heroic lawyer from *To Kill a Mockingbird*, the famed Harper Lee novel that was made into a classic American movie. The American Film Institute recently named Finch the No. 1 American film hero of all time; Gregory Peck, who played him in the 1962 feature, has called it the best role he ever had. I'm a huge fan of both the book and the picture, of Atticus Finch, and of Pat Williams, who reminded me so much of the fictional attorney.

A few years ago, I gave the eulogy at Pat's funeral. Not all that long before his death, he'd come to my fiftieth birthday party and done a memorable Mike Turpen tribute. My duties as his eulogist were far sadder, but the reason for my words about him was the same as the reason for his words about me. I was his protégé, and he was my mentor. In fact, he was partially responsible for my becoming a prosecuting attorney "way back when."

In the early seventies, I was waiting tables at a Steak and Ale restaurant in Tulsa, earning money to help pay my way through the University of Tulsa law school. That's when I first met Pat Williams. He used to come in and eat with his wife Marylen, his daughter Jenny, and his son Brian, and I'd do my best to make sure he sat at one of my tables. I'd always tell the seating hostess, "If Pat Williams comes in tonight, I want to wait on him." He was a good tipper, but far more important in my eyes was his reputation as a first-rate prosecuting attorney turned criminal-defense lawyer. I knew if I could get to know him, he could teach me a lot about the law.

I can't remember the first time I actually met Pat, but I do know that I accidentally spilled water on him—probably more than once—in my eagerness to wait on him and his family. One evening, instead of water, I spilled coffee on him—and at that point he said, "You know, you'd be a lot better as law clerk than a waiter. Why don't you go to work for me?"

I took him up on the offer. He took me under his wing, and my life was never the same after that. To paraphrase Humphrey Bogart's famous line in *Casablanca*, it was the beginning of a beautiful friendship.

I can't begin to tell you all the things Pat Williams taught me. Looking back, I believe one of his most important pieces of wisdom concerned the value of doing complete and thorough research. He used to tell me, "Mike, you'll win more cases in the law library than you ever will in the courtroom." He impressed upon me how important it was to know your case better than anyone else in the whole world so you could be relaxed and confident when you stand up in court and say, "The defense is ready, Your Honor," or "The state is ready, Your Honor."

It was valuable advice. And at first it seemed to be an unusual advice as well because it came from a guy who was an absolutely dominating figure in court. Some people still say he was the best they've ever seen. He'd become famous for the work he'd done on his feet in court, but no one—including me—really thought about the hours and hours of preparation he did before he felt he was ready to go into the courtroom. I never stopped to think how much of a part research played in his aura of confidence.

Pat begun his law career in the Osage County District Attorney's office, going from there to a job as chief prosecutor for Tulsa County District Attorney Buddy Fallis. By the time I met him, he'd left prosecution to become a criminal-defense attorney, which he would pursue with great success for the next thirty-plus years. His legacy as a prosecuting attorney, however, was an inspiration to me and a big reason I got into that profession myself.

A striking figure in the courtroom, Pat cultivated a cowboy persona right down to his hand-stitched boots. And like an Old West hero, he was a brilliant fighter who usually came out on top. Unfortunately, people like that often engender animosity and even hatred in some circles.

In 1979, while I was Muskogee County DA, Pat survived a car-bomb attempt on his life; it's still not known whether that was tied to his previous work with the Tulsa County DA's office or to something he did as a criminal lawyer. It happened around the time I was getting death threats from the Charles Troy Coleman camp, following my successful conviction of Coleman on first-degree murder charges, so I could empathize with my friend and mentor. The attempt failed because Pat had just filled up the tank of his Cadillac, and the blasting cap was triggered more by fumes than actual gas, so all it did was blow a hole in the top of his tank. Pat Williams lived to stride into courtrooms and argue cases for another quarter of a century.

In the spring 2004 issue of *Q&A*, the newsletter of the criminal-law section of the Oklahoma Bar Association, lawyer Jonathan R. Grammar eulogized Pat as "Oklahoma's prizefighter of the criminal defense bar," further noting that "his contributions to his field are unmatched." It's all true and then some. My good friend Pat Williams was a lawyer's lawyer and a memorable mentor of mine.

GIVIN' AND LIVIN'

The more you give, the more you have.

This truism has long been a motivating force in my life. Although I probably first learned it from my mother, it's actually a very Biblical principle. In the Old Testament, the prophet Malachi writes that God directs us to bring our whole tithes into the storehouse for Him, promising, in turn, to "pour out so much blessing that you will not have room enough for it." Then in the Gospel of Luke, Jesus makes his famous statement, "Give, and it will be given to you."

Some have used these and similar verses to justify what's been termed the "health and wealth gospel," the idea that if you're faithful and give money to the church, God will send financial rewards your way. I don't quite buy into that concept—it sounds a little too much like a credit-card rebate predicated on how much you buy—but I do believe that if you set aside a part of your life for serving others, you'll be rewarded with satisfaction and a richness in your life that goes far beyond finances.

The visibility of our long-running Oklahoma City–based political TV program, *Flashpoint,* has enabled Burns Hargis and me to take our show on the road, speaking at luncheons and other personal appearances (where we tend to be more humorous and less serious than we are on the show). Of course, we get an honorarium for appearing. A few years ago we both decided that instead of taking the honorarium ourselves, we'd tell whoever was cutting the check to make it out to one of our favorite charities.

Given our political and philosophical differences, Burns and I don't always agree on what constitutes a favorite charity. But you might be surprised at how frequently we *do* agree. We are, for instance, both strong supporters of Legal Aid of Oklahoma, which offers legal help for poor and disenfranchised people involved in civil cases. In 2007, the folks at Legal Aid of Oklahoma asked us to head up their annual fundraising campaign, and I'm happy to say that we were able to raise more than had ever been raised before in an Oklahoma legal-aid fund drive—well over half a million dollars.

We did it, in part, by going to the business community as well as the legal community to help organize fundraising luncheons, where we would then do our dog and pony show as a part of the effort. We helped set one of these up in Oklahoma City, asking Cliff Hudson, the CEO of Sonic, to host it. He did, and Christy Gaylord Everest—one of the most powerful and wealthiest women in the city—showed up personally, gave us five thousand dollars, and then went back and added another five thousand from her family's foundation.

We had a similar event in Tulsa, and the CEOs of major northeastern Oklahoma-based businesses came and donated thousands more to Legal Aid. Burns and I were asked to be the entertainment at still another Oklahoma City luncheon, this time for Larry Nichols, John Richels, and the Devon Energy Corporation, and we said we'd come down and give them our best stuff for thirty minutes—if they, in return, would cut a check for ten thousand dollars to Legal Aid of Oklahoma. And they did.

It was amazing. We were able to raise substantial money from people who had never given a dime to Legal Aid in their lives, mostly, I think, because they'd never known very much about it. A lot of times, by way of explanation, I'd call Legal Aid a "civil Gideon," referring to the famous Supreme Court case of *Gideon v. Wainwright*, which gave the poor the right to an attorney in criminal cases. Legal Aid, I'd tell people, does the same thing for civil cases.

What if someone without the means to hire an attorney is getting unfairly kicked out of his or her house? What if a person is threatened with foreclosure? Who helps that person hang onto a home? It's Legal Aid that empowers people to be able to stand up for themselves. As I like to say, people who are legally powerless become legally powerful with Legal Aid. And I am proud to say that the chairs for the last two fundraising campaigns have been Governor Mary

Fallin and First Gentleman Wade Christensen, and Attorney General Scott Pruitt, respectively.

We all know that when you give of your time, your talents, or your money, you receive a great deal of satisfaction in the knowledge that you've done something good for someone else. But sometimes, getting involved in giving can also change your own perception. Another of my favorite truisms is the one about how personal contact alters opinions, and while I illustrate it in this book with examples of how people began to act around Charles Troy Coleman, the murderer, it can also refer to positive situations.

For instance, I have to concede that a lot of my Republican acquaintances, some of whom I used to rant and rave about, have turned out to be very generous people. Many of us Democrats have long characterized Republicans as penurious Ebenezer Scrooge types, whose attitude toward others—especially the needy—could be expressed by the harsh old statement, "Root hog, or die." Time and again, however, I've watched my Republican friends defy expectations and come through with donations and other support for charities I'm involved with.

When people say to me, "You're raising money from *Republicans*?" I give them the line from the famed bank robber Willie Sutton. When he was asked why he robbed banks, he said, "That's where all the money is."

I got razzed in Oklahoma City because the Gaylords—a famously Republican family that runs the famously Republican newspaper, the *Daily Oklahoman*—gave us our first million dollars toward transforming an old Oklahoma City Humpty Dumpty grocery store into an academy designed to give young people topnotch professional training in the art of professional theater. People say, "Well, I guess now you can't criticize the *Daily Oklahoman* as much as you used to."

Of course I can. But the truth is it's become a better and more balanced newspaper. It's moderated a lot. Maybe, in some way, we've had a little bit of an impact on it ourselves. Certainly, the Gaylords have had an impact on me with their generosity and the good things we've been able to do together in conjunction with the Lyric Theatre, Oklahoma's professional musical theater company.

Aubrey McClendon, then the CEO of Chesapeake Energy, gave us a million dollars as well, as did the generous Inasmuch Foundation run by Bill and Bob Ross. Their contributions helped mightily with renovations on the long-standing Plaza Theatre, a part of the same wide-reaching Lyric Theatre project. Recently, Aubrey said on *Flashpoint*, "Turpen taught me to pitch a big tent, politically. Yes, I'm a Republican, but you might say I'm in flux, because I'm a natural-gas seller, and I understand global warming, and I know natural gas is the bridge to the future." And last year Aubrey successfully launched American Energy Partners, a true testament to his irrepressible, indefatigable and enterprising nature. Through our personal contact, we've had an effect on one another that is beneficial to both. Certainly, as with the Gaylord family, his million-dollar donation gave a huge boost to the Lyric capital campaign,

The Lyric project began in the fall of 2004, after the forty-year-old theater company had moved to the Plaza District of Oklahoma City. Once a thriving main-street area boasting the first air-conditioned movie palace in Oklahoma, the Plaza District had become, like many other downtown areas across the country, a mostly blighted area rife with sad, abandoned buildings.

When the Lyric Theater moved in, it acquired several of those structures, including the former Humpty Dumpty store and the old Plaza Theatre, and began a capital campaign to raise ten million dollars. The money was aimed toward renovating, operating, and endowing the theater, changing it into a venue for Lyric-sponsored live performances, and completing the educational academy housed in the former grocery store. I was asked to be chairman of the capital campaign.

What a daunting task! I wasn't at all sure we could raise *ten million dollars*.

But we did. That old grocery was transformed into the Thelma Gaylord Academy, and just down the street, in late 2007, the theater reopened with a full slate of productions on its schedule. At the academy, the kids learn to break the silence of a room with the sound of their voices—something that will help them in the classroom, the courtroom, the boardroom, wherever they choose to go. And now those kids and the academy are part of a revitalized Plaza District, a newly minted destination neighborhood for art, entertainment, and education. My good friends Tom and Lisa Price helped us reach the finish line. Generous Oklahomans like Harold Hamm,

CEO of Continental Resources; Tom Ward, CEO of Sandridge Energy; George Records, Founder and Chairman of MidFirst Bank; as well as Bill Anoatubby, Governor of the Chickasaw Nation; all stepped forward to put the landing gears on our unique and ambitious project. It took the vision of city and state leaders as well as many, many generous pledges by individual and corporate donors to make the Plaza project work. And the incomparable Lee Allan Smith helped guide my most successful odyssey for philanthropic requests.

I like to think that I represented everyone who contributed when I was honored with the John Kirkpatrick Award at the Lyric Theater's 2006 Broadway Ball. Named after the Lyric's founder and first president, the award is not given often, which made it even more special. So did the presence of my wife Susan, my daughter Sarah, and my mother Marge at the ceremony. I thought it proper, given the theatrical setting, to introduce them as the three leading ladies in my life. During the program, Sarah (dressed as *My Fair Lady's* Eliza Doolittle) sang "Wouldn't It Be Loverly" to me and then came out again as a sailor as she and other boys and girls from the Thelma Gaylord Academy sang a version of "Anything Goes" with lyrics changed to "Only Mike Turpen Knows."

What a night. It had taken a great deal of time, effort, and money from many, many people to make the Lyric Theatre project a reality. And on that night, as I stood and listened to those kids singing me a classic Cole Porter number with a twist, I felt once again how true those axioms are.

If you ain't givin', you ain't livin'. And the more you're giving, the more you have.

Campaigning for Oklahoma Attorney General in Bob
Shahan's inimitable Turpen Time Truck, 1982.

CREATE NEW REALITIES

Challenge injustice.

My first job out of the University of Tulsa Law School was legal advisor to the Muskogee Police Department. I'd gone to Muskogee to serve with Julian Fite, one of my mentors, who'd become the new Muskogee County district attorney. The legal-advisor position called for me to ride with local police officers, visiting crime scenes firsthand, and reading the Miranda Warning—the list of a suspect's rights—to those who'd been caught.

After a while, something began to trouble me about the whole procedure. We'd be stepping over the victims' bodies—figuratively speaking, but sometimes *literally*—in order to read the Miranda Warning to the suspect. We never went over to a man who'd just had his home burglarized and said, "Well, here are *your* rights as a God-fearing, law-abiding Oklahoman." We never went over to a woman who'd just been raped and said, "By the way, here are *your* rights as the victim of a crime."

To me, it all led to one thing: the system was out of balance, and it needed to be fixed. I related one of the cases that got me thinking to the *Tulsa World's* Rob Martindale a few years later. It concerned a rape victim who'd been threatened with a lawsuit from a hospital because she couldn't pay the bill for the treatment she received after she was raped. In a story he wrote for the July 6, 1980, issue of the paper, I told Martindale, "Geez, here is a woman who was an unwilling victim of crime, and she's about to become a defendant. She has sent me the bill and begged me to pay it. So what do I have to tell her? Well, I've got funds for the poor jailed rapist if he needs medical help, but I don't have any for her."

I saw it as a serious imbalance in the criminal-justice system, which insisted that we go out of our way to religiously read a suspect his rights but had no provisions for any rights that the victim might have. And as I studied all of this more, I saw this approach permeating the entire system, from the arrest of the alleged perpetrator through the pretrial, trial, and sentencing phases and beyond to such things as parole and prerelease programs. There was only one conclusion—our criminal justice system was, in reality, a criminal injustice system, one that provided for the rights of the criminal but ignored the victim.

By the time I talked to Martindale for his story, I had become DA of Muskogee County as well as the president of the Oklahoma District Attorneys Association. I used the weight of those positions to launch what became a revolutionary idea for our state: the victim bill of rights.

I'm proud to say that because of our efforts, Oklahoma was on the cutting edge of what became known during the early eighties as the victim rights movement, something I still believe was in many ways analogous to the civil rights movement of two decades earlier. With the passage into law of Oklahoma Victim Bill of Rights, which I put together, our state became a leader in the movement, and I became a national spokesman for victim's rights. To this good day, I've spoken about the topic in forty-four states, using the victim bill of rights we crafted in Oklahoma as a model of fairness and a way to make sure the system remains just.

One of the major provisions in my victim bill of rights was the victim compensation fund. And I'm proud to say that since the bill became law, we've given more than seventy-five million dollars to innocent victims of violent crime—at no cost to the taxpayer— because convicted criminals pay into a victim compensation fund.

The victim compensation fund was one of seven parts in my original victim bill of rights. Two parts—one assured a victim a speedy trial and another increased the number of judges on the Oklahoma Court of Criminal Appeals from three to nine—failed to win approval from the legislature. The other four did, however, and here they are.

- Son of Sam statute: prohibits a convict from profiting from his crime by writing a book, movie, or articles about it. This section was named after convicted New York mass murderer David Berkowitz, who, in the late seventies, got a fifty-thousand-dollar advance from a publisher to write about the killings.
- Witness Protection statute: sets a ten-year sentence for people convicted of attempting to intimidate a witness.
- Right to be Informed statute: provides parole and prison-release information to victims concerning those who performed criminal acts against them.
- Victim-Witness statute: offers district-attorney districts of over sixty thousand population the opportunity to have a victim-witness coordinator to give victims assistance in court matters.

Collected under the victim bill of rights heading, those five pieces of legislation became law in 1981 after my right-hand man, Richard Guse, and I walked the halls at the state capitol wearing our Victims Are People buttons and got it pushed through. Richard had a chillingly personal stake in the legislation—his daughter, then nine years old, had been one of the three girls killed in the heinous 1977 Girl Scout camp murders outside Locust Grove. He recently retired from his position as chairman of the state's victims compensation board, after serving for more than twenty years.

Because of Richard and many other people who saw the need to balance the scales of justice, the new idea that came to me many years ago ultimately became a new reality, one that has provided help to hundreds—if not thousands—of innocent crime victims in our state. The victim's rights movement has continued to spread across the country, and it gives me a sense of pride to know the idea that grew out of my first law-enforcement job helped put Oklahoma squarely in the victim-rights forefront, where it remains.

My dad, Wallace Kendall Turpen, World War II paratrooper who parachuted behind enemy lines in the invasion of southern France and received the Bronze Star Medal for bravery.

TGIM: THANK GOODNESS IT'S MONDAY

Destiny doesn't make house calls.

I've already outlived my father, a three-packs-a-day smoker who died of lung cancer at age fifty-three. Wallace Kendall Turpen supported his family by running printing presses, and he was good at it. He was a professional printer who believed in leaving nothing blank. I have a list of Mahatma Gandhi's "Seven Social Sins" on the back of my law-firm calling cards, where most people have nothing but white space.

Dad's main employer was Warren Petroleum Company in Tulsa, back when that city was widely known as the Oil Capital of the World. He'd been a Warren employee for more than twenty-seven years when he passed away. But he always had about five different part-time jobs as well. He would go in after hours, often very late at night, and do printing jobs for companies like Draughon's School of Business and Service Drilling.

I never saw anyone work so hard—and I was often there to see him work firsthand. He'd take me along to all these different printing sites and show me what he did. He thought maybe I'd want to be a printer someday, and he wanted me to learn his craft. (While I never became a printer, my older brother Brent did work at that profession for a time.)

The truth was Ken Turpen worked so many part-time jobs that if you wanted to be with him at all, you went with him when he did his evening and night work. That fact, more than anything else, is why I accompanied him so often.

What does a son pick up from a father who works all the time? Not surprisingly, what I came away with was an appreciation of the work ethic. It was very important to him. It was visible every day in his life. He was a true working-class hero. Although I didn't think about it consciously then, I can now look back and see how his adherence to hard work began to influence me while I was still a kid.

I took a *Tulsa World* paper route. I sold Christmas cards door to door every year and won a lot of prizes doing it. Spudnuts, the doughnuts made with potato flour, were a big thing then, and I loaded dozens upon dozens of them on my bicycle and hauled them all around north Tulsa, selling them to stores and private homes alike.

I learned a lot from Dad. And one of the biggest things I learned was what many of us baby boomers learned from their Depression-era parents—you've got to get up every morning and go to work because nobody's going to give you anything you don't earn. As I often tell my own kids, destiny does not make house calls. And over the years, all of that has evolved into one of my driving philosophies—TGIM, or Thank Goodness It's Monday.

My old man was hardly one dimensional in his influence on me. A member of the first graduating class at Will Rogers High School, he was in every musical the school had staged and remained a good amateur singer almost to the end of his days. When my brothers and I were growing up, he'd put Broadway tunes on the stereo and sing along. He introduced the family to classical music too—if a musical-theater number wasn't coming out of the home-stereo speakers, then it was likely to be Tchaikovsky's *Fifth Concerto*.

Ken Turpen was also a wizard on the tennis court, teaching his boys and our friends to play correctly, calm and patient with us, but adamant about doing it the right way. He was a fine pool player, an animal lover, a man who appreciated big cars with lots of chrome, like Packards and Buicks. And as my childhood friend Gordo Ewing recalled recently, he had "the driest sense of humor on the planet."

On top of all that, improbably, he was a first-class figure skater, good enough to be an ice-skating instructor for the Tulsa Figure Skating Club, where he was also a regular performer in the organization's annual Ice Travaganza. One of my favorite photos from my youth shows my dad, my older brother Brent, and me in a dragon outfit getting ready to perform at one of those events. What we did was skate out onto the rink in the costume to the strains of Peter, Paul & Mary's "Puff, the Magic Dragon," and then my little brother, Frosty, came out and chopped the dragon up, and we all skated off our separate ways. It was a real showstopper.

So there's no doubt that Ken Turpen, this working-class hero father of mine, was multidimensional. But one of the dimensions of his life and personality was darker than the others, and that has to be considered in any true portrait of the man.

Much of it went back to World War II. A paratrooper who served with both the 101st Airborne Division and the 517th Paratroop Infantry, he was involved in the invasion of southern France about ninety days after D-Day. He'd gotten a Dear John letter from his girlfriend and had volunteered for what was essentially a suicide mission. Instead of dying though, he ended up getting the Bronze Star for heroic achievement in action—the citation read, in part, "Pfc. Turpen fought heroically, displaying remarkable devotion to duty"—and also survived combat in Italy, Belgium, and Germany before returning home.

When he was finally discharged, however, he came home with what's now referred to as posttraumatic stress disorder. Back then, it was called other things, including "survivor's guilt," a very accurate term in my dad's case. Sometimes, after a few drinks—and he *was* a drinking man—he'd begin questioning why he'd survived the invasion when so many around him had fallen. "All those men who had families back home," he'd say. "They'd shown me the pictures of their wives and kids and then gone out and died the next day. Why was *I* spared?"

That too had a profound effect on me. Ever since then, when this country gets into a new war, I think of him and about who's responsible for sending our men and women into combat. Most of the men of my generation, the baby boomers, have never been in a war. They didn't have to serve in Vietnam for a variety of reasons, from student deferments to good luck in the draft lottery. And now those same men are responsible for sending our young people out to fight and sometimes die in foreign lands. Republican or Democrat, it doesn't matter—because they've never been there, they can't truly understand war nor survivor's guilt. In fact, some of them seem to have a romantic notion of combat, which makes it easier for them to send kids into it.

My dad knew there was nothing romantic about war. In some ways, he came back from his World War II experiences a broken man, addicted to alcohol and tobacco. And sometimes, when he'd get all wrapped up in demon rum late in the evening, a deep depression would wash over him, and he'd say, "I should've died when I was a pup."

That was a chilling statement to me then, and it still is.

Ken Turpen had many facets to his character, and I learned from them all. He was a hardworking man who got up early, stayed on the job late, and never gave up in the face of adversity. He was also an inspiration in other ways, teaching his family to love classical music and Broadway tunes and figure skating. But sometimes, memories of the war and the hardships of life caught up with him, and he lamented that he should have died young.

To this good day, it makes me feel bad that he ever felt as awful as that. But I feel blessed that I seem to have inherited his positive traits. I don't think there's a chance in the world—no matter how dire the circumstances or how beaten down I might get—that I could ever utter the phrase, "should've died when I was a pup." Every day of his life, Dad taught his kids by example to get up every morning, get to work, and get it done. I came to relish the opportunity to work long and hard at things I believed in, building on the bedrock of my father's lifelong devotion to doing as much as he could in a working day, and then get up and do it all over again the next day. And the next.

For me, that became TGIM, Thank Goodness It's Monday. There's a lot to accomplish during this life on earth, so let's get out there and *do it!* Wallace Kendall Turpen—my hard-working, flawed, inspirational, dad—left a legacy that can change your life.

SADDLE UP TO YOUR FEARS

Courage is being scared, but saddling up anyway.

—John Wayne

In an interview for the December 7, 1979, issue of the *Tulsa World*, I told reporter Doug Hicks that fear was an intrinsic part of any prosecutor's job. I was Muskogee County DA then, and like every prosecuting attorney, from DAs to assistant prosecutors, I'd received death threats from people who didn't like the way I was doing my job. And you had to take those threats seriously, even when you didn't know why they were being made or who was making them. It's something that comes with the territory.

While I was Muskogee DA, I once took a call at home from the police department, telling me that there's been a call for me. This anonymous caller—anonymity, by the way, is seldom an indication of trustworthiness—said that he could solve a murder we were investigating in Muskogee County, but that he only wanted to talk to me and only at the police station.

I decided not to take the bait, and I stayed home. Two weeks later, one of my informants told me, "Mike, if you'd made that trip, you would've been killed."

Not knowing who hates you enough to be capable of murdering you can be frustrating—and scary as well. But you saddle up anyway because if you don't, and they're able to intimidate you even a little bit, it's a victory for *them*.

As bad as it is to hear from unidentified people who want you dead, it can be just as unsettling when you know who's gunning for you. That was the case in April of '79, when Charles Troy Coleman escaped from the Muskogee County Jail.

I was prosecuting Coleman for the heinous double murder of John and Roxie Seward. One winter night, they'd dropped by the rural Muskogee home of Dell and Delphia Warren, who was John's sister. The Warrens weren't there, but Coleman was. When they surprised him as he was burglarizing the house, he forced them into the basement, and with a .28 gauge pump shotgun, he turned the room into a human slaughterhouse. He murdered them both, and when we caught him, he had their wallets, their driver's licenses, and even beef from their freezer in his pickup.

So he's in the Muskogee County Jail, and he cuts a hole in the roof and escapes—but not before telling a cellmate that the first thing he's going to do is find me, tie me to a tree out in the woods where no one can see or hear me, leave me for three days, and then come back and kill me. So when he went on the lam, I couldn't help but be a little concerned.

Obviously, he didn't find me. But he *did* go to Luther, Oklahoma, where he slit the throat of a cop who'd stopped him. That officer lived to testify for me in the second stage of Coleman's trial. But after handcuffing the man and leaving him to die, Coleman went out to a restaurant around Berryhill, killed *another* man, and stole his truck. He was in Arizona when he was stopped for speeding in the stolen vehicle. He overpowered that officer and had to be chased down by helicopters and all of that before being finally apprehended and brought back to Oklahoma—where we put him in a different jail.

So Coleman as well as some of his family were certainly capable of murdering the Muskogee district attorney who was seeking the death penalty for him. In fact, we got lots of reports about Coleman's old man from Creek County where he lived. He was making public threats, along the lines of "If my son dies, Turpen goes down." I have no doubt that he meant it. I don't doubt for a minute that he hated me enough to do it—and then some.

Charles Troy Coleman—victim of a sorry upbringing—was very simply a coldblooded murderer, the kind of person that's a threat to society as long as he draws a breath. I believed then, and I believe now, that the death penalty for Coleman was called for. I felt that if he were no longer alive, not only would we be safer as a society, but his fellow inmates would be safer as well.

Eventually, we were successful. After years of appeals, Charles Troy Coleman was executed on September 10, 1990, the first person to die by lethal injection in the state of Oklahoma. By that time, I was no longer in office. Drew Edmondson was Muskogee County district attorney then, and he was handling it. Even though it had been my case and my successful prosecution, I chose not to go.

Susan and I were living in Oklahoma City at the time, and as the execution date drew nearer, the threats on my life increased to the point that Robert Henry, the state attorney general, and Dave McBride, Oklahoma City's police chief, sent police to guard my house.

The evening Coleman was scheduled to be put to death, I followed the television reports leading up to his expected demise. But because he was the first one to be executed by lethal injection in the state, something went wrong. Apparently, they didn't have the method quite figured out, so it didn't go well. Finally, I went to bed, knowing this killer wasn't dead yet. And a little while later, I was suddenly awakened by a noise in the kitchen downstairs, like the roar of a chainsaw. It sounded as though someone was sawing or drilling through my back door.

I had a pistol back then, a .38 caliber that my good friend Rex Eskridge, now Muskogee police chief, had given me. I don't normally carry one, but I'd thought it prudent to do so when Coleman was on the loose back in '79 and once again around this time when the death threats had become so numerous. For some reason though, I decided not to take the gun along. Instead, I grabbed a baseball bat and started down the stairs, with that ominous *Rrrrrrrrr!* roaring through the house.

I reached the kitchen and switched on the light, bat in hand, and saw that the noise was coming from our vacuum cleaner tipped over on the floor! Somehow, the sweeper was running on its own. We had a cat and a dog, and the best Susan and I could figure was that our cat knocked it over and it somehow turned itself on. But to this day, I'm really not sure.

I found out later the kicker to all of this. The vacuum cleaner apparently started up at just about the exact time that Charles Troy Coleman finally breathed his last.

That threatening noise, waking me up out of a sound sleep on the night a man I put on death row was finally executed, hit me with a scary several moments. Sometimes, when I think about it, it still does. But— as the Duke suggested—I saddled up anyway, just as I had throughout all the days of Coleman's trial and sentencing.

I believe it's just something you have to do.

Oklahoma State University
Commencement
May 8, 2010

Celebration of Sean Turpen's graduation from
Oklahoma State University, May, 2010. Pictured are
Sean, me and OSU President, V. Burns Hargis.

HUMBLE TO BE LIKED

Accomplish enough to be respected, but be
humble enough to be liked.

In 1986, I announced my candidacy for governor of
Oklahoma at Tulsa's Thomas Gilcrease Junior High
School. The reason? Exactly nineteen years before, as
a ninth grader, I had become the school's first-ever
student council president. I'd gone to Monroe Junior
High in Tulsa my seventh and eighth grade years,
and then Gilcrease opened, and I spent my freshman
year there.

I remember having that exhilarating feeling of being
on a roll back then. I'd come to a brand-new school, and
the kids there had picked me, above everybody else at
Gilcrease, to be their student-council president. Things
were going very well in my young life.

But then, I began to notice that some of my friends
seemed to be feeling some jealousy toward me. It didn't
take me long to realize that in their eyes, I was getting
a little too highfalutin—a little too uppity.

I had a friend back then who became a buddy for life. His name is Gordon Ewing, and he was a consistent friend throughout those junior high years. We built model rockets and launched them together. We were close. We could talk about anything. And like many good friends, Gordo had a way of bringing me down if I was riding a little too high.

Back then, he might say, "So you beat Faye Taylor [whom I secretly admired] in an election," or, "Mary Jane Hansen's your girlfriend now." And then he'd say, "But you're still the same guy, right?"

I'd say, "Oh yeah. Yeah."

"Are you sure?"

And I'd say, "Yeah. I get what you're saying. It's going pretty good right now, but I understand. I'm still the same guy."

Later on, at McLain High School, it fell to Bill Thompson, Jackie McClure, and Johnny King to slice my parachute every once in a while. They were the ones who helped me keep things in appropriate perspective, whether it was basketball, student politics, or simply life in general.

Before high school, around the time of my junior high student-council election, I had begun putting some of my thoughts down in a diary. And one day I wrote, "Accomplish enough to be respected; be humble enough to be liked." That's one piece of life philosophy that's stayed with me ever since. With any success, I think you'd better have a good dose of self-imposed humility.

I've shared that with my kids. From the time they were old enough to grasp the ideas, I've made sure to share with them some of my favorite maxims about success: TGIM—Thank Goodness It's Monday. You've got to do something to be something. Destiny does not make house calls.

At the same time, I've always tried to impress upon them the importance of being humble. My son was on a football team that went undefeated, 14–0. They won the state championship. And I told him then, "Patrick, that's cool. Be proud of it—but be humble."

My daughter, Sarah, is the same way. She's been very successful in the theater. She's been in fifteen different shows. And I tell her, "Sarah, you're good. You're great. You're the best. You're beautiful." I heard Barbra Streisand say one day that her daddy always called her the ugly duckling of the family, so I've made a point of telling my daughter every day that she's beautiful. She's successful, and I want her to know that. But I think it's just as important for her to know that the corollary of success is humility.

My older son, Sean, has always grasped that principle. Big, strong, and athletically gifted, he has always been kind and humble—a gentle giant.

"Accomplish enough to be respected, but be humble enough to be liked" is a maxim that's served me well. I think a big part of whatever success I've had in life is the idea that you've *got* to get up on Monday morning and go accomplish something, but you have to be as humble about it as you possibly can.

Gordon, my lifelong friend, put it well: "To be able to appreciate the moment and be proud of what you have accomplished is great," he wrote me not long ago, "but to do it with humility is greatness."

TAKE A FALL

When you take a fall, take a bow.

Years ago, when I was in law school at the University of Tulsa, I was riding my bicycle through a residential area of Owasso, where my family lived at the time. It had been raining, and I didn't see the patch of mud in front of me until it was too late. The bike flipped, and I sailed over the handlebars and hit the pavement.

I looked up from where I'd landed and saw all the houses, and I just knew someone had seen me. I wasn't hurt, but I was humiliated, and thinking about somebody watching me made me feel even *more* humiliated.

So what did I do? I got to my feet and took a bow. I bowed right toward the houses, as though I'd been putting on a performance and they had been the audience.

Two weeks later, a woman saw me, and she came up and said, "Hey, did you fall off your bicycle a couple of weeks ago?"

I said, "What?"

"I was looking out my kitchen window and I saw a guy fall off a bicycle, and he got up and took a bow. Was that you?"

"Yes, ma'am, it was me."

She smiled. "I thought so," she said. "It was *you* who bowed to me."

So my whole thing is this: when you take a fall, take a bow. In other words, *never* take yourself too seriously.

Somebody might be watching.

ES, EM, ED

Every second matters.

Frosty, the youngest of the three Turpen brothers, is a very successful free-enterprise guy with a fine wife, Gayla, and three tremendous kids. Not all that long ago, he sold a company he'd built for several million dollars. As I write this, he is, among other things, president of the Owasso School Board and a man who's very engaged in the life of his community.

But well before he built his business and started his family, he was a college pitcher, attending the University of Tulsa on a baseball scholarship. A lot of the reason he was able to use baseball as a ticket to his higher education had to do with my dad, a pretty good athlete himself, who saw the potential in his youngest son, working with Frosty and helping develop his talent from early on. As I've noted in another chapter, Dad was a stickler for doing things the right way, whether it was pitching or printing, and I'm sure that some of Ken

Turpen's work ethic—and physical talent—rubbed off on his youngest son.

I like to think I had a little bit to do with Frosty's success on the mound as well. I'll swear that I can remember the particular day in our backyard when it dawned on me that he could hit either way and throw either way. I had to have been about eleven years old, so he would've been four, and I honestly think at that age I made a conscious decision to make Frosty a left-hander, believing in my young mind that it would be to his advantage. To this good day, Frosty writes and eats right-handed. But he throws left-handed, and he bats left-handed. He could have been a switch-hitter. He might have been a *switch-pitcher.* He had that kind of talent.

He was so talented, in fact, that all of the good baseball programs around Oklahoma were after him his senior year—OU, OSU, ORU. He ended up signing with TU during the time that the legendary baseball coach Gene Shell was on his way to coaching fifteen consecutive seasons at the school.

Frosty made the Golden Hurricane team as a pitcher, and to this day, he holds the record for most relief appearances in TU history. (Since the team no longer has a collegiate baseball program, that record may stand for a very long time.) He also graduated on time, got his degree, and immediately headed to Springfield, Missouri, so he could play in the Missouri Valley Tournament.

The tournament was in St. Louis, but Frosty was in Springfield because he was staying with the family of his then girlfriend, CeCe Lumpe. They had gone to TU together and graduated together.

If the name *Lumpe* sounds familiar to you, you're probably a longtime baseball fan. CeCe's dad, Jerry Lumpe, had been an all-star second baseman who'd played twelve seasons with the Yankees, A's, and Tigers. I'd met him at TU through his daughter and gotten him to autograph the Jerry Lumpe baseball cards in my collection. I was his fan.

When I heard from him just after Frosty's graduation though, it was no cause for joy. I took the call at the DA's office in Muskogee.

"Mike, this is Jerry Lumpe," he said. "Your brother was in our home this morning having breakfast, and his hand started shaking so badly that he was spilling his orange juice. He went to lie down, and he never got up. He went into a coma."

To say I was stunned would be a wild understatement. I listened in shock as Mr. Lumpe continued.

"Your brother is a big man, Mike. I had to get several people to help me, but we got him picked up and put in the car, and we drove him to the emergency room here at Cox Medical Center in Springfield. He's here now, and he's still in a coma."

Devastated, my mom and I got there as quickly as we could, only to find that nobody seemed to know what was going on with Frosty. When we entered the room at Cox Medical Center, I saw my little brother lying there, a vibrant force, a big guy, a tough guy, a bear of a man. But now he looked so fragile, motionless, with all these tubes sticking out of his body.

Gene Shell had gotten there before us, and he thought it would be best to fly Frosty back to Tulsa for treatment. But my mother didn't want to move him, and I didn't either. So we left him there and stayed with him over the next several days while he continued to lie there unmoving, unconscious.

I'm not sure whether it was the fifth or sixth day that the breakthrough happened. What I do remember is that they'd finally decided that some kind of encephalitis had infected his brain and the brain had swollen up, cutting off his oxygen and causing him to go into a coma. They told us that if he ever came out of it, he might have brain damage. He might not know who we were or where he was or even *who* he was. So on this day, I was out in the waiting room, and suddenly a door flew open and people started shouting at me. "Mike! Hurry up! Get *in* here!" I rushed in, and there was Frosty with this huge hair-dryer-looking thing on his head—a brain-scan machine—and he was writhing around, trying to pull it off. Moments before, he'd been a motionless body in a bed. Now he was a screaming juggernaut, grabbing at the brain-scan machine, ripping at the tubes stuck in his body, yelling like a madman.

I knew what they needed me to do. As I said, my little brother was a bear of man—but I'm no lightweight myself So I threw myself against him and held him down to try and keep him from jerking the tubes out or pulling the machine off his head. It was like trying to hold down King Kong, but I persevered, and finally— after what seemed to be about a week—he opened his eyes, looked at me, and shouted, *"Mike! Let me up!"*

Those were the best words I'd ever heard in my life.

While all that was going on, Frosty's teammates from the TU Golden Hurricane were in nearby St. Louis, playing in the Missouri Valley Tournament, trying to win games for Frosty because they all knew he was over in Springfield dying. But within three months of the episode I just described, he was pitching for an American Legion team at Northside Park in Tulsa. He kept the ball down and outside, and the other team couldn't hit him. Frosty won that game, and I just thought that was so cool.

Frosty eventually became a baseball coach at Broken Arrow High School and then was called by his college alma mater to coach the final team—so far—in TU baseball history. After many years as an intercollegiate sport, TU had downgraded the baseball program to club status in 1980, and Frosty was there to wind it down, routinely kicking soccer balls out of what little office he had—but still giving the program his best to the very end.

That's the way my little brother has lived his life ever since, and I think a lot of it has to do with the experience he had as a newly graduated young man, with all of life spread out before him—and then sudden inexplicable darkness. Even now, Frosty doesn't know what caused his coma or how he happened to come out of it. As I've noted, the term the doctors used was *encephalitis*, and that's about all we ever knew. But he beat it, got up, and eventually walked out of the Cox Medical Center in Springfield, Missouri, going on to live a completely normal life.

It was a life though that had changed. To this day, he can't remember much about his ordeal, including shouting "Mike! Let me up!" at me. He does, however, understand that he went through something tough, almost fatal, and survived.

He has, however, done much more than simply survive. He's gone on to become the American dream personified.

ES, EM, ED is a bit of shorthand I've drilled into my children since they were old enough to understand it. It stands for "every second, every minute, every day," and it's another cornerstone of my life's philosophy. Frosty didn't use that phrase when he beat back whatever took him down in Springfield, but he's the consummate example of living life every second, every minute, every day to the fullest. After what happened to him, I think he had the feeling of being on borrowed time. He had a sense of urgency after that—something he hadn't had before. He became a young man in a hurry—and it paid off.

As horrific as the whole incident was, it created a new awareness for my brother Frosty all those years ago. From that day forward, he has had an acute awareness of how every second truly does matter—something that sounds very simple but is actually one of the most profound ideas we'll ever encounter.

ELEVATORS GO TWO WAYS

> People are like buttons on an elevator—some
> take you up, and some bring you down.

My brother Frosty is the classic example of ES, EM,
ED—of living life to the fullest every second, every
minute, every Day. Other members of the Turpen
family also subscribe to that philosophy. My daughter,
Sarah, lives it, just like her mother and *my* mother do. In
fact, Sarah likes to share it with her friends. Everybody
in her circle is on Facebook now, on the Internet, and
they'll have ES, EM, ED up there on their Facebook
pages. Sometimes, they actually give me credit, which
is gratifying.

I introduced Sarah to the concept of ES, EM, ED
when she was very young. Her little girlfriends would
come to our house for sleepovers, and they'd see me
and say, "Mr. Turpen! Mr. Turpen! Mike! ES, EM, ED!"
They knew what it meant too.

One night, when I was putting Sarah to bed, we
were talking about ES, EM, ED. She was seven or eight

at the time, and since she had grasped the whole idea behind those six initials, I figured she was ready for the graduate course in positive thinking.

"Sarah," I said, "you've got that one down pretty well. Now I'm going to give you another one: people are like buttons on an elevator. Push some buttons, and the elevator takes you up. Push other buttons, and the elevator goes down. Do you understand what that means?"

"I think so, Dad," she returned. "It means to be positive, not negative. Like the elevator buttons, some people take you up and some people bring you down. You need to be a positive person who takes people up— not a negative person who brings people down. Is that what you mean?"

"That's exactly right, Sarah."

She thought for a moment and then asked a follow-up question I didn't expect. "But, Daddy, what about all the people who are stuck in the basement?"

I didn't expect that. Here I was giving her a simple metaphor about life, and she complicated it for me with an unexpectedly insightful question. In fact, she had me momentarily stymied. But I thought over what she said for a minute or two, and then I said, "Well, give them a helping hand, but don't get stuck down there *with* them. Don't let them bring you down. Keep your ES, EM, ED."

I'm still not sure that's the best answer I could have given her. But I'm happy to be able to say that our kids have grown up with a sense of obligation to the folks in the world's basements. They've gone all over the country on church-mission trips, helping in soup kitchens and serving the poor and disenfranchised in a number of other ways. Not many high school kids give regularly to the United Way, but Patrick and Sarah do, and they've been doing it for six straight years. They empathize. They have consciences. And Susan and I are very grateful that they do.

Really though, in some ways, what we've taught them about giving is very selfish because if you do something good for someone else, it makes *you* feel good. The more you give, the more you have. If you ain't givin', you ain't livin'.

All of that is a part of my fundamental life philosophy, something I'm given to express in maxims and metaphors as a kind of philosophical shorthand. But sometimes, it's good to have your tried-and-true pronouncements shaken up a little bit—as I did on that long-ago night, when my young daughter showed concern for the people in the basement and I had to think beyond my always-reliable sayings to find an answer for her.

The Turpen family meeting with First Lady Hillary Clinton at the White House during Easter, 1996. Frosty, Gayla, Kendal, Kelli, Susan, Sarah, Patrick and me.

DEFEATING GOOD FOLKS

I've looked at the law from both sides now.

Back in 1968, Judy Collins had the biggest hit record of her career with a song called "Both Sides Now," in which she told about moving from youthful idealism and innocence to seeing life and love from another, more mature, side. When she sang the lines, "I've looked at love from both sides now," those of us who felt we'd been down the road a bit listened to the words and sagely nodded in agreement.

As my life has gone on, I've come to realize that the "both sides now" idea doesn't just apply to affairs of the heart. I look, for instance, at the race I ran for Oklahoma attorney general back in 1982, when my opponent was the incumbent Jan Eric Cartwright. Reporter Jim Young put the contest in boxing terms for a front-page story in the *Sunday Oklahoman* of August 15, 1982.

"They're like a couple of prizefighters arguing over the booking of a championship fight," he wrote. "The 'old pro' dances away from the young contender's challenges while the 'kid' rushes around the state demanding a title shot.

"When the champ does go out among his fans he walks in with an air of confidence, is low-key in his approach and projects the image that he's getting ready to score another knockout. The contender is like a whirlwind. He races in a frenetic mood, quickly greets each person and asks for their help."

Young went on to call it "one of the best scraps Oklahoma election watchers have to view in the August 24 primaries," and he was right. It was a hell of a race. I ended up beating an incumbent who'd destroyed the opposition in the previous two Democratic primaries, a man with a very famous last name—particularly in southeastern Oklahoma—and it was because I wasn't smart enough to know that I didn't have a chance of winning.

I was still Muskogee County district attorney at the time, and I got into the race for attorney general because I thought Cartwright was going to run for governor. When he decided instead to go for another term as AG, I was stuck, so I did the best I could. I got out among the people and pleaded my case with the media, and almost before I knew it, the *Tulsa World* and the *Daily Oklahoman* were endorsing Mike Turpen. I campaigned. I worked at it, and I won. Still, when I beat him in the primary—there was only token opposition from the Republicans in the general election—it was a major, *major* political upset. Unbelievably, a local DA had beaten an incumbent attorney general.

Looking at it now though—from another side—I can see that I defeated a good man who was doing some good things. And I'm proud that once I took office, I kept almost all of his lawyers and continued fighting the same good fight that he had started. I may have beaten him for the job, but I kept his law firm working for the state because they'd been doing good work.

Cartwright died only a couple of years after our tussle for the AG nomination. But I'm happy to say that a battle he started was finished on my watch. It involved getting state control of the prison system back from federal judge Luther Bohanon, and it was one of the biggest things I accomplished during my time as state attorney general.

That brings us to another "both sides now" moment.

The prison-system case is an important one in Oklahoma history, one that dragged on for over a decade before finally being resolved. To put it as simply as I can, it grew out of a complaint filed in 1972 by an inmate named Bobby Battle, who made a number of allegations about substandard prison conditions. Battle's complaint turned into a class-action suit against the Oklahoma Corrections Department, with the inmates represented by American Civil Liberties Union lawyer Louis Bullock of Tulsa.

A couple of years later, the case found its way to US District Judge Luther Bohanon, who initially ruled that the state had to correct certain "grossly offensive" conditions. Then in 1977, Bohanon ruled that the state was not in compliance with several of his previous orders and brought Oklahoma's entire prison system under even more intense federal-court scrutiny.

Over the next few years, Bohanon mandated a number of changes in the prison system, dealing with such issues as double celling and convicts' access to courts. Ultimately, in the fall of 1983, it came down to a question of Bohanon relinquishing control of the case. Bohanon stepped out of it in November, turning the whole thing over to US District Judge Frank Seay—more than eleven years after it had begun; Seay then ruled that Oklahoma's penal facilities had been constitutional for more than a year and dismissed the case, giving the state back its prison system.

At the time, I called it a good day for the people of Oklahoma because the judge's order had given the state back the right to run its own prisons. I still believe that.

On the other hand, I can look at it from both sides now. Then, I thought that the ACLU's Bullock was a sanctimonious do-gooder and that Judge Bohanon was just looking to bang the gavel, flex his muscle, and extend federal power over Oklahoma's prison system. Along with many others, I began calling him *Warden* Bohanon because he'd taken over the state's prisons. Taking on both Bullock and Bohanon, my staff and I fought hard to get our prisons back.

Now though, I understand that Lou Bullock did what he had to do, what he believed was right—and so did Judge Bohanon. I did what I was supposed to do, but they did too. Let's be candid about this. Back in the seventies, when the prisons were under state control, they were having *riots*. There were some bad conditions. Somebody had to do something, and it was proper for Lou Bullock, on behalf of inmates, to go to court and get a federal judge involved. I think our prisons are better now because of that federal intervention. I think inmates are treated better now because of it. I've looked at law from both sides now, and I know that in this complicated and drawn-out case, we all simply did what we had to do.

United States Supreme Court, April, 1985, Ake v. Oklahoma argument. Assistant Attorney General David Lee, mother, Marge Turpen Shahan and me.

LAUGH AND LISTEN

People who never make a joke stand as a joke to
the whole world.

I've always attributed that observation to William
Shakespeare, although it may be a very loose
interpretation of something he wrote. The point,
however, has been a valid one for me—but never more
so than on November 7, 1984, when I argued a case
before the highest court in the land and injected a little
bit of humor into what were otherwise intense and
sometimes grim proceedings.

The case being argued was anything but lighthearted.
In fact, the *El Reno Daily Tribune* called it "one of the
most heinous crimes in Canadian County history."

On October 15, 1979, Glen Burton Ake and Steven
Keith Hatch stopped at the rural Okarche home of the
Rev. Richard Douglas and his wife, Marilyn. Pretending
to be lost, they pulled a pistol and shotgun on the
Douglases and their two teenaged children, bound,
gagged, and shot all four of them, and then left with

two stolen wristwatches, two wedding rings, one credit card, and less than forty dollars in cash. The wounded children played dead until the intruders left and then drove five miles to a doctor's house for help.

It was as gruesome a case as you could imagine. According to testimony from the Douglas kids, Ake had told their parents just before the shooting began, "Sorry, but I'm in a real jam here. Dead men don't talk."

Ake and Burton were tried and convicted on first-degree murder charges and sentenced to death. But after almost five years, it began to appear as though Ake would have to be retried. The American Civil Liberties Union contended that because he was indigent, Ake should have had a court-appointed psychiatrist determine whether or not he was sane at the time he committed the murders.

I was Oklahoma Attorney General in 1984 when the case finally worked its way to the United States Supreme Court. I told reporters we had an uphill battle. I was right. The ACLU was supported in the suit by national organizations of psychologists and psychiatrists, most of whom believed that indigent defendants had a right to psychiatric counsel at state expense. The central question was whether state taxpayers were obligated to pay for that psychiatric counsel in order to finance an attempt for a defendant to prove he was insane at the time of a crime.

ACLU attorney Arthur B. Spitzer and I argued before the Supreme Court on November 7, 1984, beginning at about eleven thirty in the morning. My opponent went first. At one point, Justice William

Brennan asked Spitzer if he was familiar with a certain case. He was not. I knew that Justice Brennan was going to ask me the same question, but I didn't know the case.

So Spitzer finished, and I stood up to argue. But just before I began, Chief Justice Warren Burger called for a lunch break. Along with my assistant AG and very good friend David Lee, I rushed to the library and dug up the case—which, to be fair to my opponent, was a fairly obscure one.

After lunch, it was my turn. And sure enough, Justice Brennan asked me, "Are you familiar with *Douglas v. Alabama*?"

"Well," I said, "let's be totally candid and say that I looked it up over the lunch hour."

Read the official transcript of that hearing, and what follows my statement is the term *general laughter*. I just decided I would be honest—all nine of the justices broke up, proving that Victor Borge was right when he said that laughter was the shortest distance between two people, or, in this case, nine people and me.

A few weeks later, the *New York Times* ran an article about "levity in front of the Supreme Court," using my admission as an example of how humor can work even before the highest court in the nation—*if* you're being self-effacing and spontaneous. In my case, it was sincere. I believed then—and still believe—in the communication theory that says laughter can lead to listening.

Consider Abraham Lincoln. There's a famous story about the Lincoln-Douglas debates, where Stephen A. Douglas characterized Lincoln as talking out of both sides of his mouth—in fact, he said, "My opponent, Abraham Lincoln, is two-faced!"

The sublimely homely Lincoln got up, looked at the crowd, and said, "I leave it to the audience. If I had two faces, do you think I'd be wearing this one in front of you tonight?"

For me, this is a life lesson about the value of using humor, especially at your own expense. It's quite a task to get nine Supreme Court justices to smile at the same time, much less laugh. But that's what happened when I admitted to my whereabouts over the lunch hour. I like to picture the audience at the debates laughing at Lincoln's statement as well.

Unfortunately, like Lincoln, I didn't win what I was after that time. The Supreme Court ruled in favor of the ACLU and Ake, granting him a new trial. He was convicted again, but instead of the original death penalty, the second jury gave him life in prison. That's where he is today.

His accomplice, Steven Hatch—who didn't fire any of the shots that killed the Douglases—was executed in August 1996.

And that part of the story, of course, isn't funny at all.

SECRET TO IMMORTALITY

Inscribe your name on the hearts of your fellow
man, and you shall endure forever.

E. M. Guillory, as I have stated earlier, was one of my
true mentors. I arrived in Muskogee fresh out of law
school and green as grass, having taken the job of police
legal advisor for that city. He was an older African-
American gentleman, working as an assistant district
attorney for Muskogee County. And *immediately*, this
man became my advisor.

He was in his early seventies at the time, and he was
the wise old man everybody went to for advice. Should
we file this case? Should we not file? And he'd listen
to whatever we had on our minds, and then he'd say
something like, "Well, here's the way we did it before,
and here's the way we need to do it now."

I began soliciting his opinions almost as soon as I
arrived in town. Eventually, when I became assistant
district attorney, I started working in the DA's office
with him. Then, as now, I was very passionate and

emphatic about everything I did, to the point that a few people were starting to call me out on it.

"Slow down, Mike," they'd say. "Ease up. You don't have to change the world overnight. You can't do it all yourself."

Of course, they were right in one way. I couldn't do it all by myself. But I was gung ho. I wanted to make a difference in the world, and I wanted to do it through my job. So I was one of those people who always arrive early to work; it was part of my drive and my desire to get as much done as I could, to make as much of an impact as possible.

But no matter how early I arrived at the DA's office, I never beat E. M. Guillory. He'd always have the coffee on by seven in the morning. I'd come in around seven thirty and have a cup with EM and office manager Jackye Choate, another good friend of mine.

It was during one of those early-morning sessions that Mr. Guillory first told me, "Mike, it doesn't matter if people tell you you're taking it too fast and working at it too hard. Keep that passion. Keep your purpose. Stay focused. And remember, *if you don't take it personally, don't take it at all.*" He was, among other things, letting me know that sometimes, the people who were trying to slow you down were also trying to tear you down.

E. M. Guillory practiced what he preached. He made a personal commitment to his life's work, whether it was prosecuting a case or advising someone like me. And on another memorable morning, he told me what is perhaps the most striking story I have ever heard in my life. It made such an impression on me; in fact, in 2004,

I put his words into a monograph, illustrated it with appropriate color photos, and, titling it *The Inscription*, printed and mailed copies at my own expense to people I thought would be receptive. It got lots of positive response from leaders all over the country as well as many others who understood and absorbed the power of the story and its implications.

But while I was happy to share it, the story wasn't mine. It was his. And while he said that he'd borrowed it from a Chinese mythology, I've never been able to pin down its origins. As a matter of fact, I've never heard it anywhere but from E. M. Guillory.

He told it to me one morning, after we'd sat down for our coffee.

"Mike," he began, "Let me tell you what life's all about."

You can bet that line got my attention.

He said, "A young child went to an old wise man and said, 'Old wise man, I wrote my name in the sand on the beach, and pretty soon, the tide came in and washed my name away.

"Old wise man, I carved my name in the bark on the side of a tree, and the tree grew, and my name was gone.

"Old wise man, I chiseled my name in stone on the side of a mountain, but the wind blew and eroded my name away.

"Old wise man, what really matters in this life? Can you give me a reason for living or dying?'

"The old wise man looked at the child," Guillory added, looking at me in a similarly sagacious way, "and said, 'Inscribe your name on the hearts of your fellow man, and you my child shall live and endure forever and ever and ever."

It was so simple, but so profound. It showed me that every person has the ability to add to or subtract from the happiness, the peace of mind, and the quality of every life he or she touches. It's all about how you *treat* people, how you *respect* people, how you *help* people. It's really the secret to what life's all about. Do the right thing, and you'll live forever in the hearts of those you've touched.

I've since closed my speeches with that story in forty-seven of the fifty states. I love to tell it again and again because I think it drives home in a very straightforward way a real truth about living. It's simply the most important story I ever heard. Mr. Guillory died a few years ago, and his wife asked me to give his eulogy. The service, presided over by the Rev. Ben Noble, was held at the Antioch Baptist Church in Muskogee, and I was very proud to be able to have that opportunity to speak about my friend.

Of course, I chose to tell the story he had told me all those years ago, the one I just related. And at the end, I said, "Indeed, he's left his name in the hearts of everybody in this huge, huge congregation here today."

I took it all very personally too. Just as E. M. Guillory advised me to do.

KINDNESS FOR
ADVERSARIES

Brush the chip off the other man's shoulder.

A lot has been written and said about the personal magnetism of Bill Clinton. It's something I've experienced firsthand. I've watched him shake hands, ask humbly for votes, and treat everyone he meets kindly—even those who are not predisposed to treat *him* with kindness.

Following the infamous Oklahoma City bombing, former Governor George Nigh and I spearheaded a drive to create a scholarship fund for all the kids of the people who'd died in that terrorist act. President Clinton was kind enough to accept our invitation and come to Oklahoma City for an event marking the beginning of the scholarship fund drive.

Of course, there were those at the event who were so polarized politically that they scorned the president's participation. One man in particular, who'd lost both his wife and son in the bombing, was incensed that Clinton had come, convinced that he was using the kids and the scholarships as a political vehicle to further his own career and raise his own profile.

We knew of this man's antipathy toward the president. But during the event, Bill Clinton sought him out and struck up a conversation. I wasn't sure how that was going to go since the man made no bones about being outraged by Clinton's very presence.

I couldn't hear what they were saying. But as the conversation went on, I saw the man's body language change, and I was pretty sure that the president, simply by shaking hands and being nice—being Bill Clinton— had brushed the chip off the other man's shoulder.

My hunch was confirmed when, at the end of the event, the man came up and asked me, "Do you think anyone got a picture of President Clinton and me when we were talking a while ago?" Someone had, and I'm betting the man who came to the event boiling mad about Clinton's participation still got that photograph of himself and the president framed and in a position of honor.

I thought about that a decade later, when Bill Clinton returned to Oklahoma City for ceremonies marking the ten-year anniversary of the Alfred P. Murrah Federal Building bombing. He had been president on April 19, 1995, when the heinous act occurred, and had reacted by saying, "The United States will not tolerate this. I will not allow the people of this country to be intimidated by evil cowards." Two and a half years later, he'd signed a bill authorizing the construction of the Oklahoma

City National Memorial and Museum on the bombing site, making it a part of our national parks system.

Now in 2005, he'd returned, and I was glad to have him back in town. I was watching the speakers from out in the crowd when I got a call on my cell phone. It was a Secret Service agent, who advised me that Clinton wanted to meet me backstage.

A few minutes later, in a back room, the president and I were chatting together about a lot of different things, including Hillary's thoughts about running for president. Suddenly there was a knock at the door. It cracked open, and the Democratic governor of Oklahoma looked inside. I could see he had his wife and daughters with him.

"Mike," Brad Henry said, "may I come in?"

Governor Henry knew I was close to Bill Clinton, and the governor and Clinton had just been on the podium together. Brad might want a private moment with the former president. I would, had our positions been reversed.

"Sure, Governor," I responded. "Come on in. I'll introduce you and your family to Bill Clinton."

So I made the introductions of the governor, his wife Kim, and their three daughters, Leah, Laynie, and Baylee, to Clinton, who greeted them warmly. It quickly came out that Leah was running for her class presidency at Shawnee High School, and when she asked him for advice, Bill Clinton took her hand, shook it, looked her right in the eye, and said *"Shake every hand, ask for every vote, and be nice to everyone."* That was his counsel to a budding young politician, and still I love it. It's so fundamental, so basic.

And besides, ten years earlier, also in Oklahoma City at a similar ceremony, I had seen it work quite well for him.

SECOND CHANCES

I believe in a God of second chances.

I feel sure that if you're reading this book, you know my political affiliation. At the same time, I don't want to be too partisan in these pages. I have very good friends from all across the political spectrum, and I believe far more in what unites us than what divides us. I also believe that this country is going to be a lot better off when those of us who profess to be believers stop screaming at each other and truly begin following the teachings of our Savior, Jesus Christ.

The first time Susan and I were invited to spend the night in the White House, I was in Washington, DC, to attend the induction ceremonies at the Kennedy Center Hall of Fame. President Clinton had appointed me to the Kennedy Center's Board of Directors—Susan called it Mike and the Millionaires because you had to give or raise ten thousand dollars to be on the board.

My partners on the board were high-profile people like multimillion-selling author John Grisham.

The night of the event, Susan and I rode in a motorcade to the Kennedy Center, along with the Clintons and CBS Entertainment president Leslie Moonves. CBS was televising the event.

By the time we returned to the White House, it was about one o'clock in the morning. Mr. Moonves and his wife were staying in the Lincoln Bedroom, and Susan and I were in the Queen's Bedroom, right across the hallway. We had barely gotten settled in when we heard a knock at the door.

It was Bill Clinton. He had met Queen Noor of Jordan earlier that evening, and he wanted to put her picture up in the Queen's Bedroom. It didn't take us long to see that this was the energetic, nocturnal Clinton we'd heard about. After he hung the picture, he asked if we'd like a tour of the White House. Within a few minutes, the Moonves were roused as well, and the four of us were shown around by the president of the United States in the small hours of the morning.

Clinton had just become the first two-term Democratic president since Franklin Roosevelt, a fact I pointed out to him as he took us through room after room of the White House.

"I know," he said, "but I wish we'd taken at least one house of Congress." He paused for a moment in our tour. "Democrats," he said, "want government to work. We want it to work for the people, and so we're busy with governing. They're tougher than we are. I worry because they've got both houses, and now they just might begin investigating."

Not long afterward, the investigations began. After months of intense and bitter investigations at taxpayer expense, Bill Clinton was impeached on December 19, 1998, by the House of Representatives on almost a straight party-line vote, with only three Democratic Representatives voting with all the House Republicans for impeachment.

We shouldn't forget that throughout the whole impeachment process, President Clinton's poll numbers continued to rise. Right up until his acquittal by the US Senate on February 12, 1999, it became increasingly clear that this partisan attempt to run him to the ground was not the will of the American people.

He said as much when Susan and I met with him in Oklahoma, a year or so after he'd been exonerated. Whenever he came to our state, I assembled a group of people to go out to Tinker Air Force Base and meet with him on Air Force One, which I still consider a very high honor. So here he was in Oklahoma, late in his second term, after going through all this hell and surviving. And there, aboard Air Force One, he told Susan, "Thank God the American people stuck with me."

He'd made it through impeachment. He was no longer complaining about his tormentors as he had had in our previous conversations. He was trying to move past that, to see the positive, to make the most of this second chance. Knowing that, I brought along a sermon recently given by Dr. Michael Anderson, my pastor and friend, at Westminster Presbyterian Church in Oklahoma City. It dealt with several reasons we know there is a God and how His transforming power is available at any stage of our lives.

I handed the sermon to Bill Clinton and said, "Take this, and read it on the plane."

He nodded and turned to hand it to the guy beside him. The president always has someone like that with him, a recipient of books and mementos.

But I stopped him. "No," I said, "you *read* this." And I stuck it in the pocket of his sports coat. I almost treated him like my brother, and I felt as though I knew him well enough to do that. I'm not intimating that we were hanging out together all the time, but I felt like I'd earned the right to be that familiar. I'd defended him in the national media, raised funds for him, stayed hitched to him, etc. In fact, when Hillary visited our house later on, one of the things she told us was, "Nobody stuck with us through thick and thin more than Mike and Susan Turpen."

Anyway, I shoved the sermon in his pocket and told him to read it. And two weeks later, I got a note from him on White House stationery, asking me to pass an enclosed handwritten note to my pastor. The second note read:

> *Dear Dr. Anderson,*
>
> *My friend Mike Turpen gave me a copy of your 'God Talk' sermon. I thought it was perhaps the best short statement on why we believers believe I have ever read. The older I get, the more elation and disappointment I experience in my own life*

and in the world outside it, the more I believe in 'the assurance of things hoped for, the conviction of things unseen.' Thank God for unconditional love and for second chances.

Sincerely,

Bill Clinton

As you might imagine, my pastor had that letter framed, and it now hangs in his den. But the important thing about this whole story is that the belief in a God of second chances can make a powerful difference in your life. It has in mine, and it has in Bill Clinton's life.

The OKC Memorial & Museum Board of Trustees with First Lady Laura Bush at the Memorial, 2011.

The OKC Memorial & Museum Board of Trustees with President Bill Clinton in the Museum, 2010.

UNLOCKING HORNS

You don't have to see eye to eye on every issue
to work together.

—George H. W. Bush

We live in contentious and divisive times, where never-ending blasts of politically motivated vitriol explode from our radios and TVs and slam with teeth-jarring ferocity into our email. Division along political lines is nothing new for this country, and neither are the fervor, passion, and even anger.

Now, however, anyone with a computer can throw gasoline onto the fire with simply a few keystrokes, and at any hour of the day or night, some bloviator or another can be found bellowing madly about the opposition on numerous television channels and radio frequencies. In this overloaded atmosphere, public civility and restraint—never easy propositions—become even tougher.

That's why I so admire the work of two ex-presidents: Republican George H. W. Bush and Democrat Bill

Clinton. Their appearances together on behalf of worthy causes demonstrate how people with very different political beliefs can come together for the common good. In 2004, they helped raise a billion dollars for the country of Indonesia, following the devastating tsunami there. Here at home, they partnered to help rebuild schools, libraries, and housing, following the natural disasters in New Orleans, and went on to assist hurricane and storm victims in other parts of the country. All this come from two men who ran against one another for the highest office in America in 1992, locking horns and fighting hard, each believing in his own heart he was the best man for the country.

On May 2, 2009, Clinton and Bush appeared in Tulsa to help raise funds at the annual William Booth Society dinner. It worked very well too. Nearly one thousand people shelled out some serious money for the event—a general-admission ticket cost $125—with Tulsa's Salvation Army chapter ending up with somewhere around a half million dollars for its very necessary meals and emergency-services programs.

It was a magical night, with Bush summing up the spirit of the ex-presidents' partnership when he said, "Just because you run against each other doesn't mean you're enemies. We think it sends a message that politics doesn't have to be mean."

That's the same message Burns Hargis and I tried to convey all the years we did *Flashpoint*, our weekly political show on KFOR, Channel 4, in Oklahoma City. My friend Burns left the show after becoming president of Oklahoma State University, but former

Oklahoma City mayor Kirk Humphreys has been a worthy successor—committed, as I am, to the idea of civility, even when we are poles apart politically and philosophically.

Bill Clinton made his own speech in Tulsa as well, and one of the things he said not only reinforced the idea of civility between political rivals but also gave a unique peek behind the curtains of the Oval Office.

"Typically," he said, "the president who is leaving office will think of two or three things he thinks the successor should know and, if he cares about something, particularly if there's a change of parties, says, 'I hope you will not undo this.'"

Clinton revealed that President Bush's request to him was to keep and support the Points of Light Foundation, the nonprofit organization begun during Bush's administration. Clinton not only kept it, he doubled the federal funding for it. Then when Clinton was leaving office, he asked *his* successor, President Bush's son, to reauthorize the AmeriCorps program, which Clinton began in 1992. George W. Bush honored his request and even added funding.

It's interesting to speculate, isn't it, on what George W. Bush asked President Obama to do. Not many people know. *I* don't, but I am told that AT&T CEO Randall Stephenson has a pretty good idea.

Hearing that little bit of insider's knowledge was a fascinating part of the evening for me. But I'd be lying if I didn't say that the favorite thing I heard that night was Bill Clinton introducing me as "my great friend, Mike Turpen."

My affection for Bill and Hillary Clinton runs all through this book. I value their friendship as well as the times I've been able to sit back and visit with one or both of them. I was honored to be the state's campaign manager for Hillary's presidential run in 2008, when she carried Oklahoma in the Democratic primary. (Afterward, Bill sent me one of his favorite saxophones as, he wrote, "a *small* expression of my undying gratitude for all your support for Hillary.") Each year, I am honored to join President Clinton at the Clinton Global Initiative in New York, where leaders from all over meet to work on solutions for some of the world's toughest problems.

On the evening of the Salvation Army event in Tulsa, I motorcaded with him from Oklahoma City. Earlier that day, he'd spoken at a function at the Oklahoma City National Memorial and Museum, where we'd made him an honorary board member. From the very beginning, he's been a great supporter of the memorial, and I'm happy to do my own part by serving as chairman of its development committee. I was pleased that I was able to help get my friend Bill Clinton not only to Oklahoma City, but to Tulsa as well, for two very worthwhile events.

Clinton talked about his Oklahoma City appearance at the Salvation Army dinner that night, acknowledging the award we'd given him earlier—crafted from a piece of wood from a tree that survived the bombing, with some marble from the Alfred P. Murrah Federal Building. He believed, he told us, "the way the people of Oklahoma City and the people of this state responded to that tragedy broke a fever in America." That fever had to do with the acrimony between the left and the right, the Democrats and the Republicans, which had seemed to come to a head in the mid-1990s. As Clinton put it, "We got to a point in America where we thought our differences were more important than what we had in common."

His point was that it took one of the worst acts of domestic terrorism in history to change that dark and combative national mood to get us to overlook our differences and unite. And I couldn't help thinking that now, some fifteen years down the road, the old divides, the old disagreements, the old conflicts, seem to be boiling over again.

This time, I pray it doesn't take another bombing to unite us. I pray instead that the examples of camaraderie and congeniality—despite political differences—I saw George H. W. Bush and Bill Clinton exhibit that night in Tulsa will help us on a new path away from hatred and ugliness and toward reconciliation and respect for one another, regardless of politics, race, religion, or social status. We don't have to agree. We do have to get along.

Susan and I greeting President Bill Clinton at Tinker
Air Force Base upon his arrival to Oklahoma City.

FAITH-FILLED QUIETNESS

Sometimes, you just have to let go and let God.

Here's something I want to admit to you right up front: I'm no fan of televangelists, and I do get sick of hearing people, whether they're in the public eye or not, go on and on about their religion. So I was a little concerned as this book came together because I ended up including a lot of spiritual stories from my own life.

Hypocritical? Maybe you could make that case. On the other hand, I believe deeply and unshakably that people should live their faith instead of just *talking* about it. Whatever your religion is, I think it's of utmost importance to turn your theology into biography, to use your theological beliefs in the shaping of your daily life. And when I write about faith and spirituality in these pages, it's always in conjunction with how a belief was *lived*—not just talked about.

That brings us to the case of Eunice "Sally" B. Ross as well as to one of my favorite passages of Scripture,

Matthew 7: 24–27. In the verses, Jesus is up on the mountain, speaking to the multitudes, and he says:

> Therefore everyone who hears these words of mine and puts them into practice is like a wise man who built his house on the rock. The rain came down, the streams rose, and the winds blew and beat against that house; yet it did not fall, because it had its foundation on the rock.
>
> But everyone who hears these words of mine and does not put them into practice is like a foolish man who built his house on sand. The rain came down, the streams rose, and the winds blew and beat against that house, and it fell with a great crash.
>
> Matthew 7:24–27 (NIV)

Sally Ross was a spiritual person, a devout Christian. She built her house on rock, not sand. Sally was not only able to withstand a relentless and well-financed courtroom attack on her personal character but was also able to reach even greater heights as a dedicated and committed public servant. Surely, she has made her ancestor, the famed Cherokee chief John Ross, proud.

Beginning in the early 1980s, Sally was Tahlequah's City Clerk. She was a town employee for well over a decade before that. In 1988, however, the city sued her for twenty-one thousand dollars, alleging that in 1981, she had placed her disabled husband on the city's insurance policy without getting the approval of the city council. Basically, the city alleged that she added her husband to her insurance policy without council permission, and thus the additional amount it took to pay his premium amounted to embezzlement, or formally known as misappropriating city funds.

It was a bad case and kind of a cheap shot. But they were after her politically because some of the members of the old guard in city hall were afraid she was going to run for mayor of Tahlequah. So they took the matter to a full-blown jury trial. It wasn't a criminal case, but it was an ouster proceeding, which is much the same because you're either guilty or not guilty.

When I ran for Oklahoma attorney general and won, Sally supported my candidacy. When I ran for governor and lost, she remained a loyal friend. She rode the river with me, and now, as a lawyer for Riggs Abney in Tulsa, I was there for her.

She was being tried at the Tahlequah courthouse. A few years earlier, I prosecuted the killer Charles Troy Coleman in that same room. Now I was back, this time on the defense side instead of the prosecution side. It was a heck of a feeling and a trial. The powers that be were flying people in from all over the country, former city managers, former members of the council, just so they could ask questions like, "Do you remember giving her permission to deduct that insurance premium?" Honestly, I couldn't believe it.

I don't have a transcript of my closing argument in the case, but I remember saying, "Ladies and gentlemen, everybody's against Sally Ross—everybody but the people. You. The people of this county believe she's doing a good job, but we've got some city-hall politics going on. They want Sally Ross out because they're afraid she may run for mayor, and they can't control her because she's her own person. What you see is what you get with Sally Ross."

Although there was no doubt in my mind that Sally deserved complete exoneration, I thought I was in trouble with the case. They had stacked the deck against us so heavily, flying all these people in and getting their stories straight in order to oust her. After the closing arguments were finished, the jury went to deliberate.

It was around 5:30 p.m., and I was worn out. I drove to the first motel I could find, with the intention to crash until the next morning. I was beat up from giving everything I had to this trial, from trying to save her. I mean that literally. It wasn't a criminal proceeding where I was trying to save her freedom. But I was trying to save her reputation, which was just about as important. They wanted to take away her livelihood and, with it, any political future she might have in Cherokee County.

Instead of falling asleep, as I'd planned, I found myself at the end of my bed, in this low-end motel room, on my knees, as though the bed were an altar. And I was praying, "God, please help me on this one. What these people in the power structure are trying to do to Sally Ross is *wrong. It's* unjust! But God, I know I haven't tried the best case. They have all the witnesses. They had the money to spend, brought in people from across the country, and stacked the deck against her. I have her word, and I know she's in the right. But I need your help."

After asking for that divine intervention, I felt a certain peace. I knew that it was in the hands of the jury, as well as a far higher power, and I could do no more. So I drifted off to sleep.

When I reached the courtroom the next morning, the jury was still deliberating. The jurors had been at it from 5:30 p.m. until midnight before recessing and then took the case up again at 10:00 a.m.

Around noon, after being together for some nine hours, the jurors filed into the jury box. District Judge Jim Edmondson read the verdict.

Not guilty.

The city's two attorneys requested a poll of the jurors. Nine had voted not guilty, with three voting guilty. Nine to three for acquittal.

Sally and I hugged each other, and she said, "Thank you, Mike Turpen. Nobody could have done what you did. You fought for me, and we won."

"Yeah," I returned. "But I was concerned. You hung in there, and I knew you were tough, a *Captain Courageous*. But they were after you."

What she said and did next stunned me. She said, "Mike, not to worry." And she handed me a crumpled piece of green construction paper with some words on it. "I had that in my hand through the whole trial," she explained. "The result was never in doubt."

I smoothed out the paper and saw that it was a poem clipped from some other source and glued onto the paper. Written by Mildred N. Hoyer and titled "About Prayer," it read:

When all has been done that can be done,
Though this, to some, may seem very odd, The
paramount need appears to be

> Just letting go, and letting God.
> It's like closing the door, wrapping oneself In a
> kind of solitary pod,
> And there in faith-filled quietness
> Just letting go, and letting God.
> No need to struggle or plead the prayer,
> For when mind and heart no longer plod,
> Amazingly, the answer comes—
> Just letting go, and letting God.

She had been almost supernaturally calm throughout the whole trial. I held one of the reasons why in my hand. It was one of the most powerful moments in my life.

"Sally," I said, laughing, "why didn't' you tell me sooner? I wouldn't have spent so much time at the motel on my knees!"

I knew, however, that the peace I'd felt after I'd finished my petition to the Almighty was like the peace that the poem brought her. Both of us had let go and let God. It had just taken me a little longer.

There are a couple of postscripts to this story. First, the Tahlequah mayor at the time, James Brixey, insisted to the *Tahlequah Daily Pictorial Press* that there was no personal vendetta on his part or from any council members. Instead, he was simply heeding the counsel of Tahlequah's late city attorney.

"I had absolutely nothing to gain by doing this, and neither did the council members," he said in an official press release issued after the verdict. "It was an unpleasant task that I dreaded from the beginning." He also stated he was "shocked" by the outcome, but that he would do it all again "if it had to be done."

Sally Ross, meanwhile, did enter the mayoral race and was elected by the people of Tahlequah as their city's first-ever female mayor.

2002 Dedication of Price & Turpen Courtroom at University of Tulsa College of Law. Pictured L-R: OK Attorney General Drew Edmondson, Susan and me, Stuart II, Stephanie and Jackie Price, Sarah Turpen, Nikki Price, Linda Price, Sean Turpen, Stuart Price and United States Court of Appeals Judge Robert H. Henry.

TRIUMPH & DISASTER

If you can meet with Triumph and Disaster
And treat those two imposters just the same.

—Rudyard Kipling

Have you ever wondered why we hear poetry so much during public acknowledgments of life's passages? Showers, weddings, commencements, memorial services—all given extra texture and meaning with an appropriate verse or two. Just a few lines of a poem can say so much. Good poetry speaks to the soul. It can soothe or excite, enrich and enlighten. There's great power in poetry.

One of my own favorite poems is quite well known, Rudyard Kipling's "If." If you are able to maintain in the face of all kinds of adversity, then "you'll be a Man, my son!" I'd memorized it when I was much younger, and the night I lost the runoff for Oklahoma governor in 1986, one of its couplets came back to me. It was one of the *ifs*: "If you can meet with Triumph and Disaster/ And treat those two imposters just the same."

I thought about those lines a lot during the bleak hours following my defeat. They helped me to realize that life is centered in the middle, not in triumph *or* disaster, and that's where I should be as well. The message from Kipling's words was to stay centered, to stay focused, and trust that—as Annie sings in the Broadway musical—the sun would come out tomorrow.

Two decades later, the poem popped up again in my life and in the lives of my son Patrick and six of his closest friends. Five were sophomores at Bishop McGuinness High School and Heritage Hall High School in Oklahoma City, and one was a sophomore at the University of Oklahoma. I challenged these young men to learn "If," offering one hundred dollars to each one who could recite it to me from memory.

Why did I do this? I'm sure some of it is almost genetic and certainly cultural. As early as I can remember, my mother was reciting poetry to us. It was a Christmas tradition for all of the Turpen children to gather around Mom's feet and listen as she gave us such family favorites as "The Highwayman" and "The Night Before Christmas." Also, at their ages, these boys had a lot of ifs in their lives, and hopefully the poem would strike home, as it did with me.

I also memorized a few poems throughout my life which were a continued source of wisdom and solace. In fact, when reporter Vicki Clark came to our home to do a story for the *Oklahoma City Friday* newspaper on our poetry club, she interviewed the guys, took a picture, and then turned to me and said, "Well, Mike, can you recite poetry too?" The boys had already done

"If" for her, each one taking a few lines, and another boy had recited Teddy Roosevelt's "In the Arena," the second piece they were memorizing at the time.

"You're making these boys do all the work," she said with a smile. "Can *you* recite something for *them*?"

There weren't that many poems in my memory bank that I knew completely. But one popped into my head immediately, and since I thought it was a good teaching moment, I launched into Edwin Arlington Robinson's "Richard Cory."

> Whenever Richard Cory went down town,
> We people on the pavement looked at him.
> He was a gentleman from sole to crown,
> Clean favored and imperially slim.

I did it all, right up to the ending in which this rich immaculate man, the object of much of the town's envy, "Went home and put a bullet through his head."

And when I finished, those boys said, "Mike! That's kind of a downer."

I said, "Yes, it is, but I memorized that poem my tenth grade year at McLain High School in North Tulsa. You guys don't know the demographics, but I was on the poor side of the town, and after I absorbed that poem, I could look over at the well-to-do people on the south side and think, *Golly. Thank God for what you have, Mike, and don't ever be jealous of another man.* Since I committed that poem to memory," I told them, "I've always said that I'll take what I've got and be thankful that I have it. The man on the hill that so many people envy may look like he has it all, but he could be Richard Cory."

I know that "If" has had special meaning for at least a couple of the guys in our poetry group. In the fall of 2006, David Price contracted spinal meningitis, and after weeks of treatment in Oklahoma City's Children's Hospital, he had to undergo radiation therapy at the MD Anderson Cancer Center in Houston.

His situation was very serious; from the beginning, he faced a tough fight. Like the rest of the guys, he'd memorized "If," and he told us that he found special strength in these lines:

> If you can force your heart and nerve and sinew
> To serve your turn long after they are gone,
> And so hold on when there is nothing in you
> Except the Will which says to them: 'Hold on!'

As I told Ms. Clark for the *Oklahoma City Friday* story, "Hold on!" became a kind of mantra for our group, as David held on during the darkest periods of his struggle with the disease, times when it might have been easier to just give up. But he didn't. He triumphed. He beat spinal meningitis, and we all like to think that the poetry club and Rudyard Kipling had a little something to do with it.

The other instance of "If" figuring directly in a young man's life is far less serious. In fact, it's almost, but not quite, comical.

A member of the poetry club, Ryan Randolph, came to me one day and said he'd gotten a ticket for driving without wearing a seat belt. He'd had one on, but it was around his waist only, not around his shoulder, and so he'd been stopped and ticketed.

So I took him to traffic court. Municipal Judge Alan Synar, brother of my longtime friend, the late Mike Synar, was presiding, and he said, "Mr. Turpen, it's good to see you in my court today."

"Good to be here, Judge Synar," I returned. "We're here to enter a disposition on driving without a properly fastened seat belt."

"Sounds like a very important case, but not exactly capital punishment," he said. "What do you suggest?"

"Well, we throw ourselves on the mercy of the court. We'd like some creative disposition so this doesn't go on the young man's record. He's a good student, a good athlete, and he's even somewhat poetic."

"That's what I thought," said the judge. "You're in that poetry club I've read about."

I'm sure that Ryan had begun to suspect that the judge and I had choreographed the outcome. In fact, I'd tipped him to the idea that something like this might happen. So when Judge Synar asked him if he knew any poems by heart, he simply responded, "Yes, your honor."

"Do you know 'If' by Rudyard Kipling?"

"Yes, your honor."

"Turn around," instructed the judge, "and recite it to the courtroom."

So this kid wheeled around and, without preamble, in a confident, clear voice, launched into "If." He did not miss one phrase—not one *word*—despite the fact that he was suddenly facing about two hundred people in the court, all lined up waiting for their turns before the judge. Most of them were miffed about having to pay fines, about being in court in the first place when they'd far rather be doing something else. It was what standup comedians call a tough house. Yet, when he hit the "you'll be a Man, my son!" at the end, the courtroom erupted with applause. On the way back, we were talking, and I noted that Ryan, as the starting quarterback for McGuinness, had an important scrimmage that night with Midwest City.

He said, "Mike, after what I just did, that scrimmage is *nothing!*"

So one of the kids beat spinal meningitis, another beat a traffic ticket, both to a greater or lesser extent because of their memorizing "If."

It's been interesting to watch how poetry works in their lives. They all became school poets; the coach at McGuinness had them recite "If" in front of the team. After the group's inception, Governor Henry, former president Clinton, and University of Oklahoma president David Boren all sent encouraging notes to them. In 2008, the boys visited OU head coach Bob Stoops, reciting "If" to him in his office; the coach revealed not only that he was a poetry lover, but also that the couplet atop this chapter carried a deep meaning for him. (Like those in the political arena, even the most successful coach must learn to deal with both triumph and disaster.) Interestingly enough, several months before the seat-belt incident, Judge Synar told me how special he thought the poetry club was, so he was very responsive when I suggested the poetic disposition of the case.

To me, running a poetry club for these young men was simply a manifestation of the philosophy of "The more you give, the more you have"—the idea of benefiting by leaving the woodpile a little higher than you found it. Life's lessons expressed through poetry helped them to dig more deeply inside themselves for answers to life's questions and challenges.

In his 1982 book *Souls on Fire*, author and Holocaust survivor Elie Wiesel wrote the following passage about his work, which I feel is as powerful as great poetry:

> But where was I to start? The world is so vast, I shall start with the country I know best, my own. But my country is so very large, I had better start with my town; but my town, too, is large. I had best start with my street. No: My home. No: My family; never mind, I shall start with myself.

The point seems clear to me. The young men in the poetry club are all in college now—one at Rice (on a football scholarship), another at the University of Virginia, and the rest at OU. If they've been personally inspired and enriched by poetry they committed to memory, I can think of no better going-away present.

Harland and Shirley Stonecipher with Senator Hillary Clinton in our home in Oklahoma City during her run for President.

ROOF OF THE LAW

The roof of the law covers us all.

Roylia Akins believes that the law applies equally to everybody—black or white, rich or poor, young or old. He truly believes that the roof of the law covers us all, no matter our circumstances or social standing. After he was elected police chief of Hugo, the only African American in a field of a half dozen candidates, he and his antagonists eventually found that belief tested in court.

A former deputy and then under-sheriff in Hugo, Roylia was eminently qualified for the job. A majority of the city's residents apparently agreed, voting him handily into the office. In fact, he was elected twice, beginning in the mid-1980s. He served his city, and the whole state, in that capacity for the next decade. During Rolly's tenure as chief, he also was named commissioner of the Oklahoma Bureau of Narcotics and Dangerous Drugs, and appointed to the Oklahoma Public Employees Relations Board by then governor Henry Bellmon.

From day one, Rolly did a good, tough job. But in 1995, he ran afoul of a powerful businessman who wanted him to prosecute some teenagers who were cruising around his building and parking across the street. The businessman was white; the youths were black. For some, there were racial overtones to the disagreement. Under the law, however, the youthful cruisers were not committing any crimes, so Rolly refused to prosecute them. A firm but fair guy, he was simply doing what he thought was right, refusing to kowtow to a someone else's law-enforcement agenda.

As you might imagine, this didn't sit well with the businessman, and he had a lot of influential friends in the community. Ultimately, when Rolly couldn't be persuaded to fall into line, he was relieved of his duties. The Hugo city manager, newly appointed, presented him with a letter of termination.

We'll leave Rolly's story there for just a moment, while I tell you about another good friend of mine, Harland Stonecipher.

Back in 1982, when I was running for attorney general of Oklahoma, I walked and talked my way through the whole state, going store to store, door to door. During those campaign days, I came upon a business in Ada called Pre-Paid Legal Services. It was run by Harland, who'd started off as a teacher and debate coach over in Chandler before moving to Okmulgee. In 1969, he had a car wreck, and while it wasn't his fault, the cost of the basic legal services required to get everything straightened out drove him very nearly to financial ruin. This experience gave him the idea to launch Pre-Paid

Legal Services Inc., which offers prepaid legal coverage that gives average citizens access to top lawyers. It's a concept that had been kicking around in Europe for a while, but Harland is the visionary who started it here, and he's had huge success with his company.

We hit it off immediately, and he helped me in my successful quest to become attorney general. Then, in '86, he supported me for governor. A year later, after I'd lost the primary runoff and had just set up my law practice, he walked into my Tulsa office and asked, "Would your firm be the provider for Pre-Paid Legal's twenty-five thousand members in Oklahoma?" So Riggs, Abney, Neal, Turpen, Orbison, and Lewis began a relationship with Pre-Paid Legal Services that has helped us grow from a team of eighteen lawyers to one of the largest firms in the state, with more than one hundred attorneys on our staff.

I like to say that when I got beaten for the governorship, a few good friends came walking in while everybody else was walking out. Harland Stonecipher was one of those friends. He's a man who believes in the principle of staying hitched, of helping your friends whether they're up or down, and he helped me immeasurably in getting my law practice started by bringing his company to our firm. To this day, I speak regularly at Pre-Paid Legal's national conventions—they're in fifty states and four provinces of Canada now.

To tie things back together, Rolly Akins was a Pre-Paid Legal Services member when he was unfairly ousted from his job as Hugo's police chief.

After his termination, Rolly contacted Pre-Paid Legal, and a very competent young lawyer of ours, Melvin C. Hall, began working up the case. It took a year and a half to get to trial, and throughout all that time, the other side never made any offer to settle, even during the mandatory settlement conference. Apparently, those lined up against Rolly wanted their day in court.

If that's true, they got their wish, although I'm sure it didn't turn out the way they wanted. The day arrived when Melvin and Rolly were seated against their opposition in Federal District Court in Muskogee, with Judge Frank Seay presiding. Melvin, knowing that I was a former Muskogee DA and therefore knew a lot of the people in the county, asked me to come down and help him with the jury selection, which I was happy to do. I was also slated to give the opening statement.

But just as I approached the jury to begin, a funny thing happened. The defense lawyer, representing the City of Hugo, held up a legal pad so I could see it. On the top page, he'd written the words *CAN* WE *TALK?*

Now, keep in mind, the jury was already seated. With the first word of my opening statement, the trial would be underway.

After another glance at the handwritten question on the legal pad, I asked, "Judge, can we approach the bench?" He told us to make it quick.

I said, "Judge, they want to talk."

So he gave us ten minutes, and we went out into the hallway with the opposition's lawyers. They offered us a very substantial amount of money (the exact amount is still protected by a confidential settlement agreement) to pull the plug on the whole case—a lot of money to keep me from ever making that opening statement.

We took it.

In an infomercial for Pre-Paid Legal that runs regularly on the Court TV network, Rolly says that even if he didn't receive a penny from the settlement, it would still have been worth the long process "to get back my dignity and the fact I could walk back into Hugo, the folks knowing I was not guilty of any wrongdoing."

In addition, he says, he "wanted to do something to see if the people of Hugo still respected Rolly Atkins," so he ran for the city council—and won.

That's not the end of the story. The council ended up appointing Rolly mayor of Hugo. The city manager who'd given Rolly the letter of termination was himself terminated. And Rolly served as Hugo's mayor until he retired from politics. Currently, he's the full-time pastor at Hugo Chapel Church.

I think the axiom that begins this chapter can be interpreted to mean that the law not only *applies* to everyone, but it also *protects* everyone. Rolly's job as police chief, and the way he performed his duties, pitted him against some powerful people. But the law applied to those folks, even as it protected Rolly Akins. The roof covers us all—even those who might think they're above it. Give an assist, however, to Pre-Paid Legal Services, Inc., which still includes Rolly Akins as one of its card-carrying members. According to Rolly, it always will.

My family celebrating my induction into the Oklahoma Hall of Fame, 2010. Pictured: Sean, Susan, Sarah, Patrick and me. A really big night.

LIFE GOES ON

Stay gold.

—Johnny Cade to Ponyboy Curtis in S. E.
Hinton's novel *The Outsiders*

Some say that *The Outsiders*, written by my fellow Oklahoman Susie Hinton, was the first true young-adult novel ever written. Certainly, this tale of youthful class conflicts—which has sold millions of copies and spawned an award-winning movie directed by Francis Ford Coppola—is one of the best-known young-adult books of all time, still speaking its truths to legions of readers more than forty years after its initial publication.

Part of the genius of the novel lies in Hinton's thematic use of Robert Frost's poem "Nothing Gold Can Stay."

> Nature's first green is gold
> Her hardest hue to hold
> Her early leaf's a flower;
> But only so an hour.

Then leaf subsides to leaf
So Eden sank to grief
So dawn goes down to day.
Nothing gold can stay.

In *The Outsiders*, gold is used to symbolize youthfulness and innocence and a sense of wonder, things that we often shed as we grow up. Some of it, indeed, can't stay, at least not in its original form. But my wife, Susan, and I, have spent our life together striving to disprove the great American poet Frost. We have long approached our marriage with those two words: stay gold.

I have in my files a letter Susan wrote in the mid-eighties, when we were first dating. I had sent her a copy of "Nothing Gold Can Stay," and she'd responded by saying she found it "short, simple, and somewhat sad," but that she, like S. E. Hinton's character Ponyboy, felt that it was important to try to "stay gold."

"To me," she wrote about the poem, "it is a reminder that the new always fades, diminishes, etc." But, she added, with some concerted effort, "You can renew the sheen of that priceless golden treasure." When she wrote that, we were several years away from getting married, and I'm not sure either of us thought much about it at the time. We both had fulfilling, busy lives. I was Oklahoma's attorney general, gearing up for my hard run at the Democratic nomination for governor, and Susan was a vocational-education instructor at Emerson Alternative School, an inner-city education center for pregnant teenagers. She was a first-class educator, loved by her students, and she valued and cherished her time with them.

Rosa Parks, an inspiration to us both, once said, "We must stand up for the children, just like I sat down for freedom." Susan was doing just that with her job. For years, she helped scores of students, mostly from disadvantaged backgrounds, get good educations and good jobs.

Today she is back in the classroom at the incredible U.S. Grant High school, but Susan was working at Emerson when we met, after I was asked to give the school's commencement address. Our meeting turned into a friendship, which led to romance. We dated for five years before I finally popped the question, and it was in a memorable setting.

Susan and I had flown together to Kauai, Hawaii, in late 1989, where I was to give the keynote address to a meeting of the National Association of Attorneys General. She didn't know that the contents of my luggage included a ring, along with a legal memo prepared by our firm's legal intern George Emerson. Its title? "How to Get Married in Hawaii."

The night before I was to speak to the group, we went to a luau (where we partook of the powerful island specialty known as a Blue Hawaiian), and when we were alone, I gave her a shoebox package. She unwrapped it, found the ring inside, and looked at me with some amazement. That's when I gave her George's memo.

"Susan," I said, "you're a schoolteacher. You're good at working out details. So why don't you work out the details and let's get married?"

Hawaii had a three-day waiting period for marriages, and we were on a five-day trip, so we ended up getting married on Dec. 6. It could have also been the next day, but both of us were aware that Dec. 7 was the date the Japanese attacked Pearl Harbor, and Susan was adamant about not getting married on Pearl Harbor Day.

"Well," I said, "at least we'd always be able to remember our anniversary."

Warren Price, Hawaii's attorney general at the time, located a courtroom and a judge for us, and on December 6, we were married by Judge John "Spike" Matsuka, with my friend Steve Clark, attorney general of Arkansas, as an official witness. Another friend, Bob Abrams, was New York's attorney general and the president of the National Association of Attorneys General. He declared the official state dinner, held as part of the proceedings, to be our wedding reception.

The day after the wedding, I gave my speech, titled "Is There Life after Politics?" I began the presentation by talking about the words of author Robert Frost in "Nothing Gold Can Stay." Asked about the most important thing he'd learned in his eight decades of life, Frost responded that it could be summed up in three words: "Life goes on."

Only a few years earlier, I told them, I'd been beaten for governor and had left public life to join the Riggs Abney law firm in Oklahoma City. "Life *does* go on," I said. "Now I'm in private practice, it's thriving, and I was married yesterday at the Kauai courthouse!"

Well before we were married, Susan and I both understood that neither of us, nor anyone else, is perfect. And we both subscribed to Ben Franklin's adage about courtship and marriage: "Eyes wide open before and half-shut after." Still, to turn around the title of a famous Shakespearean play, we also believe "all's well that begins well,"

Our marriage, with its romantic island setting, certainly began well. You could call it the perfect beginning to a perfect marriage. As I like to say (humorously, of course), "Susan and I have a perfect marriage. I don't try to run her life, and I don't try to run mine either."

Sometimes, when a speech calls for it, I publicly advocate five three-word phrases that every man should use in order to maintain marital bliss and harmony:

I love you.

You look beautiful.

Let's eat out.

Can I help?

(Drum roll, please) It's my fault.

Once, when I relayed those bits of wisdom while speaking to a Pre-Paid Legal convention in Las Vegas—attended by more than five thousand PPL associates—Susan stood up after I was finished and sliced my parachute by saying simply, "Mike needs to practice what he preaches!" It brought the house down.

Susan left teaching in 1990 to raise our family, and she's excelled in that arena as well. Most recently, in addition to teaching a confirmation class and serving on the membership and evangelism team at our church, she was named Super Mom at the Bishop McGuiness football banquet. Following in his older brother's successful football footsteps, our son Patrick was a member of the team, which went 39–3 during his three high school years. Susan contributed in any number of ways, including arranging meals for the team's road trips, decorating the buses, and making sure motivational magnets were on every player's locker before each game. She was, so to speak, coach Kenny Young's right-hand mom.

Susan is the best mother in the universe, and that's just part of the reason I think so highly of her. She is my partner in everything I do. Throughout our years together, she has continually come through for the rest of the family and me, always polishing and shining up our lives and our relationships, always doing her best to ensure that she and those around her can stay gold.

Life, indeed, goes on. Thankfully, I have Susan to share it with.

THINK OF ME NOT

> Don't worry about what other people think about you. Truth is, they don't think much about you at all.

That maxim comes from my good friend and television partner for more than fifteen years, Burns Hargis, who ascribes it to his dad. Burns and I began co-hosting the political talk show *Flashpoint* over Oklahoma City's KFOR-TV following the 1992 presidential election—just about five years after the box-office blockbuster *Dirty Dancing* hit America's screens.

What does a piece of wisdom from Burns's father and a top movie from 1987 have to do with one another? In my particular life history, they're definitely linked, although it will take a bit of explanation to pull everything together.

You might recall that the stars of *Dirty Dancing*, Jennifer Grey and Patrick Swayze, played respectively the young and inexperienced Frances "Baby" Houseman and a worldly dance instructor named Johnny Castle.

On a vacation to the Catskills with her family in the 1960s, Baby falls under the spell of Castle, who's teaching "dirty dancing" moves to summer campers. Later, Baby becomes his partner both on the dance floor and off set. The film spawned an Academy Award-winning song, "I've Had the Time of My Life," which perfectly captured the way Baby felt about her consciousness-raising romance with Castle.

For a finger-snap portion of the real-life 1960s, Shirley Eaton was my Johnny Castle. It happened one evening when we were both seventh graders. I tended to be, well, a little on the nerdy side; Shirley, on the other hand, was the queen of the hop, beautiful and popular and the object of my considerable affection. I spent a lot of time wondering what she thought about me.

Then one magical summer night, she was part of a group playing spin the bottle in Susan Fowler's backyard. When my time came to spin, the almost unthinkable came true. I spun, and when the bottle stopped, it was pointing at the most beautiful girl in Monroe Junior High School. Playing the game gave me a chance to kiss Shirley Eaton.

To this day, I can remember that night vividly, right down to the smallest details: the sounds and the smells of the evening, the stars above, the major and minor-keyed emotions that skittered through me, the way Shirley looked when our lips touched as we leaned together in the darkness, somewhere between the swing set and the doghouse. For those few moments, she was like Patrick Swayze's character in *Dirty Dancing*, teaching the ways of the world to someone with far less experience and far more anxiety.

As an adult, I would often recreate that night for my friends, describing just how deeply it touched me and how insecure and ham-handed I was in the presence of this dream come true. I'd wonder aloud about what she thought about me on that night and how it shaped her perception from that night forward.

And then I had a chance to ask Shirley Eaton herself.

It was the ten-year reunion of our McLain High School graduating class, and Shirley showed up. I immediately went over and thanked her for that long-ago evening, which had been such a combination of wonder and anxiousness on my part. Curious, I asked how she remembered that momentous night in my personal history. Had I been too eager? Clumsy? Inexperienced? Had I seemed backward or unsure of myself?

I described the evening in detail. I named names, pointing out the other participants. I fixed that moment in time for us both.

And as much as I tried, I still could not elicit a single observation from her about that night. She wasn't trying to be mean or above it all. She simply had no memory of what had happened or how she had perceived me before, during, or after that kiss. It was obvious that, as Burns's dad put it, she hadn't thought much about me at all.

Elsewhere in this book, there's a quote from a Tom Brokaw speech about how adult life is a lot like junior high school. It's true. You never really grow out of it. By the time Shirley and I met at the reunion, the intensity that had marked my insecure seventh-grade days was long behind me. Somewhere deep in the back of my mind, however, an emotional residue from junior high remained, still lingering fifteen years after our backyard kiss. It made me a little sad when I finally realized that no effort on my part could make her remember.

Now, many years later, I realize that meeting up with Shirley again led to a valuable life lesson and a perfect illustration of the wisdom of Mr. Hargis's advice. Different things are important to different people, and what we think and feel—our inner lives, with all their joys and insecurities, questions and notions, memories and perceptions—are by nature far more important to us than they are to anyone else, simply because they're our own.

HOLD THAT DREAM

Thank God for unanswered prayers.

Oklahoma's own Garth Brooks became the best-selling pop music recording star of the 1990s, as well as one of the biggest country music acts ever, in part because of his ability to get to the hearts of his listeners, to give a voice to the truths and emotions that live deep inside most people. Take his no. 1 hit from 1990, "Unanswered Prayers," for instance. Is there a one of us who, at one time or another, hasn't thanked God that certain dreams and prayers, large or small, *didn't* come true?

As I've written elsewhere in this book, being governor of Oklahoma was a big dream of mine that tumbled to the ground and shattered into painful shards after the 1986 Democratic runoff election. But because that prayer of mine wasn't answered, I ended up marrying my dream girl, Susan, starting a family, and helping build the law firm of Riggs, Abney, Neal, Turpen, Orbison & Lewis. I had been single, trying to change the world, off on a quest like Don Quixote—

and then, it all changed. Although it hurt deeply at the time, and it took a while for the scars to heal, losing that runoff was the best thing that could have happened to me.

It might be stretching things a bit to call Charlie Hanger's request a prayer or even a dream. But it definitely was something he wanted. An Oklahoma State trooper as well as my friend, Charlie contacted me in the early 1990s when I was in private practice. He asked me if I could do anything to help him obtain a transfer. He was working Interstate 35 around Oklahoma City, and he wanted to move to the Cimarron Turnpike. He felt that the change in assignment would allow him to spend more time with his family.

I phoned contacts in one of the best law-enforcement organizations in the country, the Oklahoma Highway Patrol, but to no avail. Finally, I told him, "Charlie, unfortunately I can't help you."

So he stayed on I-35. And not long afterward, on the morning of April 19, 1995, his eye caught a 1977 Mercury Marquis rolling down that interstate—one with a bare patch where a license plate should have been.

April 19, of course, was the date of the infamous bombing of the Murrah Building in Oklahoma, and Charlie had actually been called to Oklahoma City for assistance earlier that morning. But while he was still on the way to the city via I-35, orders came in rescinding the assignment and requesting him to stay in his own area. It was on a northern stretch of I-35 that he stopped the yellow Mercury.

This happened around 10:20 a.m., and the events surrounding the destruction of the Murrah Building were still being sorted out. So Charlie wasn't looking for the perpetrator of the horrific crime. He was, however, extra cautious as he approached the vehicle, thinking about a recent shooting not far from the spot that involved another officer.

The other driver got out of the car, meeting Charlie on the highway's shoulder. According to the May 15, 2001 edition of *Capitol Network News*, Trooper Hanger first asked the man why he didn't have a tag and was told that the car was a new purchase. Then Charlie asked to see a bill of sale and was told that it was still being filled out by the previous owner. Charlie asked for an insurance verification form, but the driver had none.

Finally, Charlie asked for a driver's license. "It was at this moment," states the *Capitol Network News* story, "that Hanger became a part of history."

When the man reached into his back pocket for his billfold, his jacket tightened enough for Charlie to see a suspicious bulge under his arm. Charlie told him to open his jacket with both hands. As the man began unzipping the jacket, he admitted to having a gun on his person. Charlie grabbed the shoulder holster he spotted under the man's jacket and removed a .45 caliber weapon, dropping it onto the side of the road and telling the man to put his hands in the air. Then Charlie drew his own gun.

Before it was all over, Charlie had also confiscated an ammo clip, a knife, an envelope full of antigovernment rants, and a copy of the novel *The Turner Diaries*, in which a truck bomb blows up a federal building. More important, he had Timothy McVeigh, who would later be convicted and executed as the primary figure in the Murrah Building bombing.

"I think he was a coward in that he didn't want to confront someone that was armed, because he had ambushed the people he had killed," Charlie told the *Capitol Network News* reporter. "They didn't have a chance to defend themselves. I don't think he wanted to put himself in a situation that would put him in danger."

Now Charlie Hanger was an experienced trooper, and officers with experience notice things like a bulge under a jacket. They also know how to deal with an armed suspect. Because of his skill and intelligence as a law-enforcement officer, Charlie was able to disarm and subdue the biggest mass murderer in American history. He quickly became a hero, the man who captured Timothy McVeigh.

But think for a moment. What if I'd been able to get Charlie the transfer he wanted? Someone else would've been working that stretch of I-35 that day, and it could have been a person with less experience and less savvy than this veteran lawman. It's conceivable that McVeigh could have left another law-enforcement officer lying on the highway. He might have gotten away. He might *still* be on the loose.

Charlie Hanger is Noble County sheriff now, up in Perry, Oklahoma. I have no doubt that he still gets interview requests from newspapers, magazines, radio, and TV about that day on I-35 when he was all that stood between the Oklahoma City bomber and a clean getaway. He has, after all, become a towering figure in the history of our state.

And sometimes, I know, he must be thinking about what would've happened if his wish had come true way back when, and he'd been patrolling the Cimarron Turnpike, like he wanted, on that black day in Oklahoma City.

Prayers, wishes, dreams, requests—sometimes it turns out best not just for us, but for the people around us, if they remain unanswered.

One of my favorite pictures--daughter Sarah and me at a Father's Day luncheon, 2009.

FATHERS & DAUGHTERS

> The best thing that can happen for women in
> our society is for men to have daughters.
>
> —Sheila Birnbaum

I've had the privilege of representing a number of
Fortune 500 companies run by good folks who pay
on time. Once, when I was advocating for State Farm
Insurance, I was in a strategy session with a high-
powered group, including former New York attorney
general Bob Abrams, former Kansas AG Bob Stephan,
former Iowa AG Bonnie Campbell, and the preeminent
Sheila Birnbaum, a well-known New York-based
corporate counsel.

During our meeting, I told them a story about Sarah,
my daughter, and something she'd said to me when we
were watching *The Sandlot* together. That 1993 film,
you may recall, is about a young boy learning to play
baseball in his new neighborhood; there's a game going,
and one of the boys says, "You play like a girl!"

That's when Sarah yelled at the TV screen, "Well, what's wrong with *that*?" She really didn't get the slur at all. Not only was her mom very athletic, but we had also been discussing the then-recent triumph of the USA over China in the 1999 Women's World Cup. As I told the rest of the group, to Sarah, playing like a girl was a compliment. To me, it showed that we had come a long way since *The Sandlot*'s release.

"You're right," Sheila said. "And the best thing that can happen for women in our society is for men to have daughters."

I will never forget that statement. It helped me to understand my abiding respect for all of the women in my life who have knocked down barriers and built bridges for Sarah to walk across.

These women include US Secretary of State Hillary Clinton, who has been in our home twice—once as a US Senate candidate and the other during her presidential campaign. Except for my mom, Marge, my wife, Susan, and Sarah, Hillary Clinton is the most talented and wonderful woman I have ever met. She inspires, she empathizes, she leads. We are pleased to count her as a family friend and look forward to her positive impact during her service as America's ambassador to the world.

I am also close to Governor Brad Henry and his wife, Kim, who was gracious and made a difference during her time as Oklahoma's first lady. I love the story *The Oklahoman*'s Jane Glenn Cannon wrote about her back in 2007. Referring to Kim's childhood, Cannon said, "As the only girl and sister to three rowdy brothers, Kim knew the rules: Don't Cry. Don't tell. Eat fast. Keep up or be left behind." Kim and another good friend, former Tulsa mayor Kathy Taylor, have served the people with courage and class. And our current governor, Mary Fallin, is Oklahoma's first woman governor.

My aunt Mildred was our Auntie Mame, a larger-than-life maestro of good times. Her daughters Leah, Molly, and Nancy continued in her footsteps. The other Turpen gals—Gayla, Kendal, and Kelli—are also filled with life, love, and enthusiasm. As are Mary Lou, Christina, and Julie. Shirley Stonecipher and Kay Watson helped build big companies and better lives for countless people. Paula Stover and Gail Beals at the Lyric Theatre and Kari Watkins, and our inspirational leader Polly Nichols at the Oklahoma City National Memorial and Museum, and Judy Love and Deborah McAuliffe Senner at Allied Arts have all taught me about passion and purpose. Educators Elsie Rains, Arlene Hinkley, Ramadeen Roller Phipps, Paulette Braden, and Cheryl Skalnik helped shape my life in most significant ways. I am inspired by the work of Nicole Nash at the Hannah Senesh Community Day School in Brooklyn, NY. Jackye Choate, Jean Jackson, Susan Cochran, and Sheila Williams helped run and organize my life in my various vocations in Muskogee and Oklahoma City.

These are the women of my life: my leading ladies—Marge, Susan, and Sarah—and all the others who have inspired me and helped make the world better, fairer, and more compassionate—a place where Sarah, and all the daughters from all its corners, have a better chance to thrive and succeed.

Senator Joe Lieberman, Connecticut U.S. Senator, presenting me at the 2010 Oklahoma Hall of Fame Induction Ceremony. Joe and I were state attorneys general together.

MOMENTUM & NOMENTUM

He's got that quality I like in people: he likes me.

In 1982, when I was Oklahoma's attorney general, Joe Lieberman was the attorney general from Connecticut, and we got to know each other. A couple of decades later, when he was seeking the presidency of the United States, he gave me a call.

"Mike," he said, "I need you to support me," and he started going into his stands on the major issues of the day.

Before he could get very far, I stopped him. "Joe," I said, "I'm for you."

He paused. "Good. Why?"

"Because you've got that quality I like in people," I explained. "You know exactly who I am. You know *me*. And I'd rather know a president than to know *of one*. So, Joe, I'm for you. We don't agree on every issue, but I'm for you."

In this book, I've headed the major chapter on convicted killer Charles Troy Coleman with the axiom

"Personal contact alters opinions." That's because the people around Coleman, his custodians and law-enforcement officers, started seeing him as a human being instead of a coldblooded murderer. This chapter could have the same heading, but with a different spin. As I said, I hardly agreed with Joe Lieberman on all of the issues facing America and the world, but I was in his corner because I knew him. I'd had personal contact with him, I felt that he was a friend, and that counts for a lot.

This ties in with how I approach the people I meet. I know that every person is a book, and whenever you walk into a classroom or a gymnasium or a meeting hall, you're walking into a roomful of books. If you'll take a little time to read them, to show a little interest in their lives and in their feelings, they'll not only be grateful and appreciative, but you'll have learned something about *them.*

Believe me, I know I'm a talker. But I try to be a listener as well, and a good enough listener to empathize when other people express their feelings. You don't have to ask profound questions to get them to talk to you. "How are you doing?" or "What's going on?" are often enough. But when you talk to people—and listen—you're making personal contact with them. You're reading pages in the books that we all write with our lives. Getting to know someone, even a little, alters opinions, and the alteration is almost always positive. The people you take the time to "hear" will feel that they know you, and you'll know them better as well. You'll be showing a quality that most people like.

Once Joe had my endorsement, he began telling the story of our phone conversation at his stops all across the country, using it as a springboard to connect with his audiences. In a speech to, say, the National Association of Attorneys General, he might tell the crowd, "I've got a friend in Oklahoma, Mike Turpen. He's a former attorney general, and he told me that he's behind me because I have that quality he likes in people—I like *him*.

"I know Mike. I know his name. And I know all of you here. Regardless of your party affiliation, I know you. I was an attorney general myself." And there he'd go.

I gave him another line that he used on the campaign trail, one that I took from Barry Switzer. He was a supporter of Oklahoma Governor Brad Henry, and when Brad was running, Switzer would say, "We've got momentum, and they've got *no*mentum."

I told Joe about Barry's line—which probably dated back at least to Barry's fabled coaching days at the University of Oklahoma—and he said, "I like that." So he took the phrase, changed it to "Joe-mentum," and used it throughout his campaign.

On Super Bowl Sunday in 2004, Joe ended up at our house, standing by our fireplace while Sarah sang "Everything's Coming Up Roses" to him. A few weeks later, he dropped out of the presidential race, and my daughter said, "Dad, that's the guy I sang to, isn't it? I thought everything was coming up roses for him."

"Well," I returned, "they were for a while."

Joe, of course, had been the Democratic vice presidential candidate in 2000, when he and presidential candidate Al Gore actually won the popular vote but lost the election—with a substantial assist, many believe, from the US Supreme Court. And while Joe fell short four years later in his bid for president, he came back in 2006 and retook his seat in the US Senate. That was doubly tough because he ran as an independent.

So while Joe Lieberman's Joe-mentum didn't take him to the top office in the land, it's served him well in his career. And I'm proud that I can call him a good friend. After all, he's got that quality I like in people.

HITCHED TO LIFE

Forgive—and remember.

The race for the 1986 Democratic nomination for Oklahoma governor was not without its lighter moments. The six names on the Democratic primary ballot included such perennial fringe candidates as Virginia Jenner, who'd had her name legally changed to Virginia Blue Jeans Jenner, and the freelance reverend Billy Joe Clegg, who also ran several times for president—sometimes as a Democrat and other times as a Republican. His slogan was "Billy Joe Clegg won't pull your leg," and he was fond of bringing beakers to the candidates' debates and handing them out, telling us to "pee in the cup so we can see who's on drugs." (Jenner, incidentally, received more than 16,000 votes in the primary, while Clegg ended up with nearly 6,500.)

At the top, however, things were less amusing—at least for me. I'd been the state's attorney general since 1983, and I figured it was time to take another step up and run for governor. A young conservative Democrat with good law-enforcement credentials from my years as Oklahoma AG and, before that, as Muskogee County DA, I thought it was the right time to run, and a lot of other people did as well.

I was the favorite in the race. But I was ultimately beaten by David Walters, a real-estate executive and former provost at the University of Oklahoma's Health Sciences Center. I had the name recognition, but he came out of nowhere with a campaign that essentially branded me as a "career politician" and blamed me for a lot of things I had nothing to do with.

In the August 26 primary election, David took nearly 44 percent of the tally, while I had a little over 40 percent. The other four candidates split the rest, leading to a runoff between David and me.

Of course, I was deeply disappointed when I didn't win the primary outright. I felt like Abraham Lincoln in 1858, after he'd lost an Illinois senatorial election to Stephen Douglas. Asked for a comment by a newspaperman, Lincoln said he felt "like the boy that stubbed his toe—it hurt too bad to laugh, but he was too big to cry." Still, a number of my friends and confidants felt that I could come back and win in the runoff, which was just a few weeks off at the time.

So the morning after the primary, I was sitting in the office of Stuart Price, the oil-and-gas man, who'd been my de facto treasurer in Tulsa during the campaign. Fairly glum, I remember how he told me to hang in there. I recall another friend, Richard Mildren—who's now my law partner—sitting at the table, saying, "C'mon, Mike. Let's go try to *win* this thing." Ed Edmondson was there, giving the same kind of encouragement.

There was another guy at the table, another member of my team. When Stuart started talking about the money we needed to be raising for the runoff and handed out a printed agenda, this man spoke up and said, "Well, you know, Walters has got all the momentum. I think maybe you should just get in there and support him now and pay off your debt. This is going to be a bloody runoff. He's got the money. He's got the momentum. And you don't."

In retrospect, that was probably legitimate advice because I did end up with a sizable debt I had to pay off. But before I could say anything, Stuart Price reached across the table and took the sheet of paper with the agenda away from the man.

"I sense a little defeatism here," he said, looking the guy squarely in the eye. "Why don't you go on back to Oklahoma City? We've got a governor's race to win."

The man got up and left, and I haven't seen much of him since. But the rest of them stayed, and together, we planned our strategy for winning the governorship of Oklahoma.

We didn't, but we came very close—close enough that there was serious talk of a recount. When the runoff votes had all been counted, David had 235,373, or 50.43 percent, while I had 231,390, or 49.57 percent. He had won by less than one percent of the total vote— not quite four thousand out of nearly a half million ballots cast.

As I've said elsewhere, losing the runoff turned out to be one of the best things that ever happened to me because I married Susan, the woman of my dreams, we began our family, and I started to help build a law firm. Also, there's no way of knowing whether or not I could have beaten the Republican candidate and former governor, Henry Bellmon, in '86. David didn't, although he came back and moved into the governor's mansion four years later. But I truly felt that I was the best person for the job at the time. I would bring in a whole new team of people, impact Oklahoma history in a big way, and help make this state a better place to live.

I was deprived of that opportunity, and it was pretty tough, even though I took some consolation in the fact that it had ended up as one of the closest races in Oklahoma gubernatorial history. Now, looking back, I can see that while it's always good to win, it's good to lose sometimes as well—if only because you can honestly say to people in similar situations that you know how they feel.

In 2001, former Oklahoma first lady Cathy Keating failed in her bid for the Republican nomination for a seat in the US House of Representatives. Many thought she was the frontrunner, but she lost. The day after the primary, I sent her flowers with a note that said, "You lost when you were supposed to win. I know how you feel."

People don't know what to say to politicians when they lose. It's almost like a funeral. But I knew what to say because I'd been there. I'm a Democrat, she's a

Republican, but that doesn't matter. She's a good lady and a friend, and I knew how she felt.

As for Stuart Price, Ed Edmondson, Richard Mildren, and the other people around that table that morning who stayed with me—we've been fast friends ever since. We were in a foxhole together. One guy left the room, and the rest of them stayed hitched. And staying hitched—"dancing with the one that brung you," as the old saw goes—is an important part of my life philosophy. I believe that everything friendship is about is contained in those two words: stay hitched. Real friends stay hitched through better or worse, through thick and thin, like my friends in that office did the morning after the primary.

It ties in with this chapter epigraph, "Forgive—and remember." The old line is, of course, "Forgive and forget," but in politics, I think it's more important to forgive and *remember.*

We all know what hard work it is to forgive someone whom you believe has wronged you.

It wasn't any different for me. David and the people behind him had done nothing less than steal my dream, and it takes time to forgive something like that. I won't lie to you. I was hurt and angry for a long time about a lot of things having to do with that race. I never really vowed to even the score or get revenge or anything like that, but it was hard to be friends again with a lot of the people who had lined up against me. Sure, it's just politics, and everyone chooses sides in a race like mine and David's, but knowing that didn't make forgiveness any easier. I had to work every day at it for months and months.

Still, you have to forgive. There are a lot of reasons that Jesus talks so much about the importance of forgiveness, and one is that it's so hard to do. But he's very clear about it—just look at the Lord's Prayer.

On the other hand, you learn from remembering. Frankly, I would've been a chump if I'd tried to forget exactly what happened in that race, what went right and what went wrong, who rode the river with me and who didn't, who stayed hitched and helped with my comeback and who bolted. I remembered what was done to me—and who did it—in order to learn from it.

On another level though, there comes a time when you've got to let it go—and I did. David has been my friend for years now, and everybody who helped raise money for his '86 campaign—they're my friends now, every one of them.

It was a test of spiritual strength, but I've been able to forgive and move on and continue living a positive life. At the same time, I've remembered how it all went down in 1986, filing those memories under "Lessons Learned."

ETERNAL GENERAL

Faith, Family, Friends, Finances and Fitness—A
Balanced and Meaningful Life

Michigan's Frank Kelley served the state of Michigan
as attorney general for an amazing forty-two years,
holding the office for so long he was nicknamed the
Eternal General. (His successor in the office, who was
also his protégé, was Jennifer Granholm—the eventual
governor of Michigan.) Frank and I met when I was
AG of Oklahoma, and we became such good friends
that when he retired he had me come up and emcee his
retirement dinner in Detroit.

He spends his summers at Michigan's Mackinac
Island, and a few years ago, he had my entire family
up to visit. We stayed in the captain's quarters at Fort
Mackinac, which dates back to the Revolutionary War,
and he and my mother, Marge, became fast friends.
Among other points of agreement, they both believe
that eighty is the new sixty.

Although Frank became an octogenarian a few years ago, he's still a practicing attorney, continuing to do his good work for the people of Michigan.

He's also in remarkably good health. He's been swimming every day for many years, and I've always known him to take good care of himself. A little while after he'd passed the eighty-year-old mark, I asked him if he had any particular secrets for living a long, healthy, and productive life.

"Well, Mike," he confided, "it has to do with three little black books."

Of course, I wanted an explanation.

"Your first little black book is the one that has all your girlfriends in it," he said. "The second one has the names of all your clients—or, if you go into politics, the contact information for all the county coordinators of your campaigns. But at this point in my life, the most important little black book is a third one—the one that has all my doctors in it, along with their email addresses, cell phones, and home numbers. I'm serious. I have four or five good specialists who are only a phone call away."

To me, that was one of those cycle-of-life stories. You start with the little black book with the names and numbers of your ladies of interest and go from there to one with your law-practice clients or county coordinators and then start one that has the contact information for your doctors.

Somewhere, I read a maxim that encapsulates Frank's good advice: "When you're young, your body is a slave to you; when you're old, you're a slave to your body."

I speak a lot about the four Fs of a balanced, meaningful life: faith, family, friends, and finances. I call it the Mike Turpen 4F Club, and I truly believe one of life's great challenges is getting those four things balanced. Life's *really* about three of them—faith, family, and friends—but to support your faith, take care of your family, and have fun with your friends, you've got to have some money.

Over the years, Frank has heard me speak on the four Fs many times. Once, after one of those speeches, he told me, "Mike, as you get a little older, you've got to add a fifth *F*, and that's fitness. You want to stay fit enough to be around to enjoy everything else."

As a result of our conversation, I've added that fifth *F* to my philosophical equation. Frank Kelley, who takes great care of himself and keeps his little book of doctors nearby, impressed upon me the importance of fitness. And upon reflection, the admonition of my good friend Gene Rainbolt always rings true: "Mike, longevity is a great ally."

Life is terminal, of course, but we can all help our own causes by doing things like wearing seatbelts, not smoking, and making our doctors our friends. I hope doing all of that helps me to live the rest of my life as well and productively as my memorable mentor Frank Kelley.

2010 Oklahoma Hall of Fame inductees. L to R: Lew O. Ward, III, Edward F. Keller, Kristin Chenoweth, me, Judy Love and Robert A. Heffner, III.

FEEDING ANGELS

The finest form of intoxication is conversation
among good friends.

The above quote has been attributed to Winston
Churchill, a great historical figure who knew a thing or
two about intoxication. I've been fortunate in my life to
have many good friends who have believed, as Socrates
did, that the unexamined life is not worth living and
that discussing ideas is the mark of a civilized society.

During my years in the DA's office in Muskogee, I
was blessed with friends like Ben and Jackye Choate,
Jimmy and Jean Jackson, Gary & Carol Parker, and
Rex Eskridge, the city's chief of police, all of whom
always seemed to have the time to sit down and talk on
a high level.

These days, I don't have to go far to find stimulating
and thoughtful conversation. Dr. Kyle Toal and his wife,
Dr. Susan Chambers, are our next-door neighbors, and
for at least the past decade, Susan and I have gone over
to their house just about every summer Sunday evening

to resolve all the problems of the world over a meal of his superb smoked ribs, along with the occasional cool brew. Kyle is a thoracic surgeon, but he's also a great friend and spiritual advisor.

You'll recall my mentor and friend Frank Kelley's advice about keeping a little black book with all your doctors' contact information so that they're only a phone call or an email away? Well, I've taken that idea to a new level—two of *my* doctors live right next door.

Our kids—Sean, Patrick, and Sarah Turpen and John, Coralee, and Ben Toal—have grown up together. The four of us—Kyle, the two Susans, and me—have had a hand in raising each one of them. And when I look back on the wisdom and philosophy we've tried to teach them along the way, a story comes to mind, one that illustrates a concept we all think is important. It's about feeding the better angels of your nature.

> The story concerns a wise Cherokee elder. One day, he told his young grandson, "A terrible fight is going on inside me, a fight between two wolves. One wolf is jealousy, anger, bitterness, regret, pride, self-pity, and cruelty. The other is joy, peace, hope, love, truth, humility, compassion, justice, and generosity.
>
> "This battle isn't just going on inside me," he added. "It's going on in people all around us. I imagine that the wolves are also fighting in you."
>
> After considering the words, the young boy asked, "Which wolf will win, Grandfather?"
>
> The old man looked at his grandson. "The one that you feed," he answered.

Our kids probably first heard that story on one of those summer nights, sitting by the big cooker in Kyle and Susan's backyard, eating some of the best ribs in the world. As they've grown up, our children have also been the subjects of endless hours of conversation around that cooker. We've commiserated for years about their social, athletic, and academic pursuits—when we're not figuring out solutions to the world's big problems.

Kyle and I did a lot of the latter after the 2007 Fiesta Bowl. He drove out to Arizona to see the game, and I flew in with the idea of riding back with him. When people asked him why he drove all that way instead of flying, he answered them with a parody of the famous MasterCard TV ads.

"Five tanks of gas, $200," he'd say, "two speeding tickets, $150, thirteen hours in the car with Mike Turpen—priceless."

Needless to say, I was flattered by that line.

The Poetry Club meeting with University of Oklahoma football Coach Bob Stoops. Coach Stoops loves the poem IF by Rudyard Kipling and he had the young men recite it to him, 2009.

WATER GREED VS. NEED

Measure twice, saw once.

It was a classic case of environmentalists vs. industrialists, and I was right in the big middle of it. To put it simply, the Army Corps of Engineers office in Tulsa had given two Texas utility companies permission to begin constructing a pump station and pipeline that would divert water out of Lake Texoma—a huge body of water on Oklahoma's border with Texas—to hundreds of thousands of North Texas residents. The Oklahoma Wildlife Federation objected, claiming that the corps failed to undertake an environmental-impact study before issuing the permit, which allowed the utilities to ultimately pump up to seventy-five million gallons of water daily from the lake.

The Wildlife Federation people showed me what Texas was doing and asked me to represent them. Seeing it as a case of water *greed*, not water *need*, I joined their fight. On November 23, 1987, I stood before US

District Judge Thomas Brett in a Tulsa courtroom and made my opening statements.

One of those statements, picked up by several newspapers, was an axiom I'd first heard a long time before: "Measure twice, saw once."

It came from my uncle Ralph Dorsal, a carpenter, who was married to Aunt Mildred, my mother's older sister. They lived around Fifty-Sixth Street and North Lewis, near O'Brien Northside County Park, in a big two-story house with Uncle Ralph's work shed in the back. I spent a lot of time there growing up, and to this day I remember him telling me to make sure your measurements are right before you ever put a saw to a board. It's s a lot easier to double-check measurements than to throw a board away and start over because you were careless when you measured it.

As I told the court, the Texoma case was a perfect example of the corps failing to measure twice, and therefore not knowing exactly what the consequences of subsequent actions would be.

Our side was joined by the Oklahoma attorney general's office and two Texas- based environmental organizations. On the other side were the two utilities, the North Texas Municipal Water District of Wylie, Texas, and the Greater Texoma Utility Authority of Denison, Texas, along with the Corps and the United States Attorney's office.

We contended that the corps was setting a dangerous precedent by granting the utilities permission to start building without requiring a formal environmental impact statement; the other side, represented by

Assistant US Attorney Peter Bernhardt, disagreed. "The stringent and far-reaching conditions attached to the permit are more protective of the environment than the accumulation of thousands of pages on an environmental impact study could be," he said, summing up the defendants' position.

I didn't believe they were right. If they were going to pump thousands of gallons of water out of Lake Texoma down to Dallas and its environs on a daily basis, if they were going to take all this water for an indefinite amount of time, the least they could do would be to put the necessary time and effort into make an environmental impact study.

Unfortunately, Judge Brett disagreed. He ruled in their favor, the pump station was built, and to this good day, Texas is still pulling thousands of gallons of water a day out of our lake. I'd given it the best I could, but as often happens, the environmentalists lost, and the industrialists won.

Now, almost a quarter of a century after that decision, I still disagree with it, although I have nothing but the utmost respect for the now retired Judge Brett. In fact, Tom Brett was instrumental in helping us obtain over one million dollars from the Mabee Foundation for the Lyric Theater and the Oklahoma City National Memorial and Museum. I also have huge respect for my late Uncle Ralph. The Army Corps of Engineers should have taken heed of his wisdom and measured twice before they let Texas saw off, metaphorically speaking, a big unending slice of Oklahoma's water.

Oklahoma State Regents for Higher Education. Front row L-R: me, Ike Glass, Julie Carson, Chancellor Glen Johnson and Jimmy Harrell. Back row: Dr. Ron White, Jody Parker, Stuart Price, Toney Stricklin and John Massey.

BALLOON OF YOUTH

Time you enjoy wasting is not wasted time.

I want to preface this chapter with quotes from two people who mean a great deal to me. You've already met them both in this book. The first bit of wisdom comes from my mother, who told me as I grew up—and continued to tell me throughout the early part of my adulthood—"Never let go of the string on the balloon of your youth." In other words, keep your youthful enthusiasm the rest of your life. I think everyone should do that as much as it's possible. I've been able to do it in my own life, thanks in great part to my mother's reminders.

The other line is from my pastor, Mike Anderson, who once said, "God is happiest when his children are at play." What a great thing to consider: God is the happiest when we're having fun ourselves. My joyful relationship with the Oklahoma State Fair in Oklahoma City was nurtured by such wisdom.

I've taken my kids and their friends to the fair for the past decade. The break in the temperatures of the summer and the autumnal azure sky that goes with it, the incredible smells from the scores of different food stands, the faces of young boys and girls as they ride the Tilt-a-Whirl or try to win a prize at one of the booths, the dizzying array of other sights, strange and beautiful, that you won't see again until the fair rolls back around in another year—it all combines to bring out the kid in otherwise responsible adults. The Oklahoma State Fair is a journey, a safari, and it's as much about what you bring back—whether literally or figuratively—as it is about going.

For me, the single event that sums up the lure of the fair is the basketball-toss booth. You know what I'm talking about. There's a basketball goal and a row of giant stuffed animals ringed around the top of the booth, which is manned by a carny who keeps shooting balls through the hoop in a maddeningly offhand manner. For, say, three dollars a shot, you can try your own luck. Make a goal and win your choice of one of those big prizes.

Who knows how long that game has been around the fair and carnival circuit? I know it's been there ever since I can remember. As a teen at McLain High in north Tulsa, I learned to play basketball from one of the best—Coach Joe Shoulders, brother of rodeo hall of famer Jim Shoulders—but when it came to shooting goals at those booths during the Tulsa State Fair, I'd always lose my money. I'd pay a dollar at a time or two dollars at a time, and I'd take the shot and miss. I don't ever recall carrying home one of those stuffed animals. That sad, but true, teenage memory causes me to think about the coaching philosophy of Oklahoma City Thunder Coach Scott Brooks: "Tough games build tough players!"

As I grew got a bit older, a little wiser, and a little better off, I learned an important truth: scared money can't win. It's futile to put down two bucks and shoot, followed by another two bucks and another losing shot. You can *never* win that way.

What you have to do is give them a twenty-dollar bill and say, "How many shots can I get for *this*?"

They're carnies, you know. They'll cut you a deal right there on the spot. So they might say, "For twenty bucks, you can have ten shots." All of a sudden, you've improved your odds of winning, even though they're pretty sure you're going to miss every time. The thing is you have to get the rhythm, and you have to arch the shot. You can't shoot it flat. It has to be a high, arching shot for that big ball to get through that squashed rim. The odds are stacked against you, but if you step up with confidence and negotiate for more than just a couple of shots, by the fifth or sixth time, you have a good chance of getting down the rhythm and the arch! You can start hitting.

I know it sounds immodest, but over the years, I've gotten pretty good at that particular game— good enough to point several times to the display of stuffed animals and say to my son and daughter and their friends, "Pick anything you want up there—the big dog, the big lion, the big bear—anything." What a beautiful feeling it is to be able to say that.

How good did I get? I was good enough to be banned by the carnies at the Oklahoma State Fair, who refused to let me play at their booths. "No, no," they'd say, "you were the guy who was here yesterday. You've already won too many times."

To tell you the truth, it was kind of fun. We'd banter back and forth and have a good time.

Then three weeks or so after the Oklahoma State Fair one year, I went down to the OU-Texas football game in Dallas. Before it started, I wandered over to the basketball booth on the Texas State Fair grounds, looking to shoot a few. I asked the guy how many shots I could get for twenty dollars, and he started to tell me. Then a look of recognition slowly filtered into his eyes.

"*Wait* a minute," he said. "You're that guy!"

"What guy?" I asked, trying to sound innocent.

"The guy from the Oklahoma State Fair!"

"No, no," I said, "I'm from Austin."

He shook his head. "No, you're not! You're the guy who won all the bears and tried to bleed us all dry in Oklahoma City three weeks ago!"

"No, that wasn't me," I said, reaching for the ball. "I paid my money. Now let me shoot."

We went back and forth, and he wasn't about to give me a chance to win anything. Finally, my wife outed me. "Yeah," she said, "he's the guy."

"I *knew* it!" the carny said triumphantly.

Out of the thousands of people they see in their travels, that guy recognized me from the Oklahoma

State Fair. It gave me a certain sense of satisfaction or notoriety to be busted by a carnival worker. I almost expected him to shout "Hey, Rube!" the universal circus and carnival warning that something's gone badly wrong and immediate help is needed.

The coda to the story is this: after winning all those prizes for the kids—after enjoying my wasted time to the hilt—and then getting recognized in Texas, I went on TV and radio in Oklahoma City, talking about how much fun it was for me, my kids, and their friends. The next thing I knew, Clay Bennett, chairman of the magnificent NBA team the Oklahoma City Thunder and head of the Oklahoma State Fair, invited me to serve on its board of directors. I was the biggest cheerleader for the fair they could find.

The time I enjoyed wasting at the fair, matching skill and wits with the carnies at their booths, wasn't wasted time at all *because I had so much fun wasting it.*

Busted by a Texas State Fair carny, I was promoted to the Oklahoma State Fair Board of Directors. It was better than a teddy bear.

White House meeting with President Ronald Reagan
in 1985. He captivated a delegation of state attorneys
general with his sharp wit and disarming sense of humor.

POWER OF LISTENING

Every person is a book if you'll just take the time to read it.

Because this chapter is about the power of listening, I could have used several maxims to introduce it—and they're all good ones. Management consultant Jim Collins, for instance, says, "Don't be interesting—be interested." In a piece he wrote for the December 2005 issue of *Business 2.0* magazine, he recalled getting this advice from a mentor, John Gardner. Gardner, the founder of Common Cause and secretary of the Department of Health, Education, and Welfare during Lyndon Johnson's presidency, was a professor at Stanford University in his later years. At the same time, Collins was a newcomer to the faculty.

"One day early in my faculty teaching career—I think it was 1988 or 1989—Gardner sat me down," Collins recalled. "'It occurs to me, Jim, that you spend too much time trying to be interesting,' he said. 'Why don't you invest more time being interested?'"

Collins wrote that the advice changed his life in thirty seconds.

Then there's the late Fred Rogers, the Presbyterian minister who became a beloved public-television icon. His advice was "Listen to other people's feelings." It wasn't all that different from what management guru Peter F. Drucker once wrote in his *Wall Street Journal* column: "Listen first, speak last."

How about leadership guru John Maxwell, who's sold an incredible eighteen *million* books and lectured to audiences ranging from the administration of the National Football League to ambassadors at the United Nations? I was privileged to hear him speak at an event sponsored by the University of Central Oklahoma in October of 2008, and later to have lunch with him and UCO president W. Roger Webb and University of Oklahoma Athletic Director Joe Castiglione.

In his lecture, Maxwell talked about John Wooden, the fabled UCLA basketball coach, and how Wooden had said that the key to leadership was listening. At the luncheon, I asked John Maxwell what *he* thought was the no. 1 leadership quality.

He said, "Modeling—leading by example."

I then asked Roger Webb, who came up with *empathy*.

My own? It's courage. But listening is right up there as well—especially when it's something I call *active listening*. Two of the best examples I can think of happened during tense times, when much was hanging in the balance.

In the late 1990s, my friend George Mitchell—the former majority leader in the US Senate and a noted writer, lecturer, and educator—took one of the hardest jobs of his life when he agreed to chair the peace negotiations in Northern Ireland. Not many—including most of the people he met on the streets of Belfast—gave him much of a chance.

But he persevered, and the result was the 1998 Belfast Agreement signed by representatives of both the British and the Irish governments and most major Irish political parties and later ratified in a referendum by Northern Ireland voters. A historic political development, it went a long way toward ending decades of strife and bloodshed.

How did George Mitchell do it? In a story that appeared in the spring 2000 issue of *Response*, Seattle Pacific University's online magazine, staffer Connie McDougall wrote that George "found that the ability to listen was a great advantage in the talks."

"We don't often truly listen to each other. It takes concentration," Mitchell says. "I also tried to encourage them to see each other as I saw them: as fellow human beings with the same aspirations."

As one of the participants in the negotiations for the agreement had said, "He listened us out."

That's a great line. He didn't *wear* them out with arguments or ideas or lectures. He *listened* them out. George Mitchell's success in Belfast was built around the power of active listening.

In 2009, George Mitchell had another opportunity to utilize his peacemaking skills. In the early part of that year, President Obama appointed him US special envoy for Middle East peace. After I had written George a congratulatory letter, he wrote back, telling me, "I don't underestimate the difficulties. But I'm honored to be asked to again serve my country, and will do so to the best of my ability." I prayed that his involvement in this effort would bear fruit.

The other instance of active listening that comes to mind involves Janet Reno, the former attorney general of the United States of America. When the Columbine High School tragedy happened in 1999, she was still AG, and I witnessed firsthand the effect that listening can have.

On April 23–25 of that year, I was in Breckenridge, Colorado, speaking to the Denver District Attorney Training Conference on trial philosophy and techniques. The Columbine High School shootings stunned the world only a few days before, in the town of Littleton, about ninety miles east of Breckenridge. We knew that Janet Reno was coming in to talk to the school's parents and students, so several of us drove over that day. What we saw was America's attorney general—a tall, statuesque woman—walk into the high school auditorium and immediately take command. There were hundreds of people there, mostly students and distraught parents, watching her every move as she walked to the podium, pulled out a legal pad, and said, "I came today to listen to the young people."

For the next forty-five minutes, she hardly said a word. She listened, and she took notes. And by doing so, she provided a catharsis for those people because they were able to tell her how they felt, to express their frustrations and their fears to a powerful figure in the

US government. And as person after person spoke up, she continued to listen, making notes on what each one said,

It's a cliché, but in this case it was true: when those around her were losing their heads, she kept hers. That's a real challenge for anyone, but it's an important thing to be able to do because the first one to lose his head is usually the last one to find it.

On that day, Janet Reno was a perfect illustration of courage as defined by Ernest Hemingway—grace under pressure. When I visited with her afterward, I told her she had given the most powerful performance I'd ever seen during a time of crisis. She listened to me, just as she had listened to the parents and students—very composed, cool, and calm—and said, simply, "Thank you, Mike."

Two major American statesmen. One, George Mitchell, brought peace to a country. The other, Janet Reno, brought peace of mind to a grieving, angry town. People opened themselves up like books, begging to be read, and these two peacemakers did just that.

It's amazing what can be achieved simply by listening.

On the campaign trail during the 1986 race for governor. Former Oklahoma Governor and U.S. Senator Henry Bellmon and I had just finished a round of horseshoes at a 4th of July celebration in Chandler, OK.

AVOIDING RIGHT VS. LEFT

> We must think in terms of right and wrong, not right and left.

Former Oklahoma governor Henry Bellmon, one of my political heroes, can be found elsewhere in this book. He's the man who gave me the valuable advice about not having to dance every dance once you're in office.

He also said something I've tried to take to heart. Years ago, during a speech at what is now the University of Central Oklahoma, he said, "Avoid the temptation to be overly partisan."

It's never been harder. Of course, political bickering has been going on since political parties were formed in our then-new country. There were always those who made a living, or simply got a charge, out of fanning the flames of dissent and criticism. But twenty-four-hour radio, television, and online news channels have produced an overabundance of commentators who feel that the only way to make their mark—and their money—is by being more outrageous, confrontational, and louder than those on the other side of the fence. Perhaps bipartisanship has never really been the order of the day in this country, but seldom have we been more divided.

It's a struggle to remember that what we should be dealing with is right and wrong, not right and left. Frankly, it's not nearly as much fun to be reasoned and rational about, say, some of Rush Limbaugh's more outrageous statements. But Bellmon—a Republican himself—urged his audience that night to resist the temptation, and he was correct. It's the same thing David Boren, a Democrat, wrote about in his recent book, *A Letter to America.* There's simply too much partisanship, he said, and I can't disagree.

Back in April of 1985, during my run as the state's attorney general, I spoke to a big luncheon in Broken Arrow, Oklahoma. Paula Burkes Powell covered it for the *Broken Arrow Daily Ledger,* and here's how she opened her front-page piece for the paper:

> Contrasting his liberal views regarding his consumer protection efforts with his conservative pro-capital punishment stand, Oklahoma Attorney General Mike Turpen told Broken Arrowans Monday that he is concerned with what's right and wrong in Oklahoma— rather than what's on the right or left side of the political spectrum.
>
> "Everyone tries to label you liberal or conservative," Turpen said in a joint Rotary-Broken Arrow Chamber of Commerce luncheon at Indian Springs Country Club. "I believe in education, jobs and justice," the state

leader said, rebuking any attempts to tag him conservative or liberal.

Of course, it's no secret to anyone reading these words that I'm a Democrat. But I've always tried to approach my job from the perspective of what's right and what's wrong. A case in point, I believe, goes back to 2001, when Oklahoma's two Republican senators, Jim Inhofe and Don Nickles, nominated four of their fellow party members for district judgeships in the state. One of the nominees was Joe Heaton, who went to the same church I did in Oklahoma City. Another was Steve Friot, also from OKC, whose wife taught my daughter. There was Claire Eagan, in Tulsa, who then had the opportunity to become the first woman ever to serve as a judge in the northern district. The other nominee was Muskogee's Jim Payne, one of my favorite judges of all time, who helped me by coming forward with powerful testimony back in the late 1970s, when I prosecuted a local judge in my role as district attorney (a story found elsewhere in these pages).

I often found myself in disagreement with Senators Nickles and Inhofe on a variety of policy issues but had a great deal of respect for the individuals they chose to fill the judicial vacancies in our state. And that's exactly what I said in an endorsement letter I wrote and mailed to several US senators, including majority leader Tom Daschle, judiciary committee chairman Patrick Leahy, and my friend Hillary Rodham Clinton—all Democrats. The four nominees may have been from the opposing political party, but they were four good people, and I believe that the letters I wrote helped expedite their confirmation.

A few months later, someone showed one of those letters to Senior US District Judge Ralph J. Thompson, a hugely influential man in our part of the world. In Oklahoma City, where he's headquartered, we affectionately and respectfully refer to him as the Judgemaker. He's a man who knows how the system works. And he picked up the phone and called me.

"Mike," he said, "what you did for those judges with that letter is the most statesmanlike thing I've ever seen."

I've always been flattered that someone of his stature thought enough of what I did to ring me up and say what he said. It's one of the nicest phone calls I've ever received.

A few years later, I had the opportunity to do the same thing for Jerome A. Holmes, who had been nominated by George W. Bush and supported by Republican senators Inhofe and Tom Coburn for a judgeship on the Tenth Circuit Court of Appeals. Again, Holmes was a Republican. But because I happened to know him, believe in him, and respect him—as was the case with the four earlier judges—I once again sent a letter of recommendation to Democratic members of the US Senate, who would, of course, be either confirming or rejecting him. In my concluding paragraph, I wrote, "Jerome enjoys widespread support among Oklahoma Democrats and Republicans alike ... He is a dedicated professional who would be committed as a judge to fairness and justice, rather than ideology."

Jerome, however, had a little harder time of it than his four predecessors. Many Democrats, as well as civil rights groups, objected to his nomination because of newspaper opinion pieces he'd written regarding such things as affirmative-action programs, the death penalty, and jury composition.

After much debate and scrutiny though, Jerome Holmes ended up as the first African American on the Tenth Circuit Court of Appeals. He was by no means a shoo-in. The vote was 67–30, and only a dozen of those voting for his confirmation were Democrats. Did my letter help sway any of those twelve senators? I don't know, but it apparently impressed Inhofe, who has never been a particular fan of mine, nor of Democrats in general. During the debate over Holmes on the Senate floor, Inhofe said this about me: "He is a very partisan Democrat. I don't think he has ever said anything nice about a Republican in his life except Jerome Holmes."

Of course, Mr. Inhofe was simply indulging in a bit of characteristic hyperbole to make his point. Jerome Holmes made his own point in a different way when he himself wrote me a letter, thanking me for "repeatedly and strongly" supporting him and expressing gratitude for my letters to the senators on his behalf. All I was trying to do was think in terms of right and wrong, not right and left, and then act on my decision in a positive way. And while it takes a considerable suspension of my disbelief to say this, perhaps Senator Inhofe was simply using different words to do the same thing.

Hosting NBA Commissioner David Stern, and his
wife Dianne, at a Thunder-Grizzlies play-off game in
Oklahoma City, 2012. Thunder Up America.

MOOT MEMORIES

> You can always tell where people are going if
> you know where they came from.

You'll find other words in this book about my very
good friend Stuart Price and the way he unwaveringly
rode the river with me during my campaign for the
governorship of Oklahoma. Stuart also figures into
something else I'm very proud of—the William
Stuart Price and Michael C. Turpen Courtroom at the
University of Tulsa College of Law. Formally dedicated
on April 15, 2003, it's used for public meetings and,
occasionally, real court proceedings. But it primarily
functions as a model courtroom—technically called a
moot courtroom, a place where law students can go to
learn how to try cases.

I first started attending law school when it was
located in downtown Tulsa. Then the school moved to
John Rogers Hall on the TU campus. That's where I first
encountered the learning opportunities available with a
moot courtroom. In 1974, my senior year, I participated

in a moot-court competition in that very room, arguing my case in front of a three-judge panel. There were three of us on my team—Bob Sullivan, who went on to a job at the Grand River Dam Authority; Neil Wallace, from New York; and me—and we did well enough to be chosen to represent TU at the Regional Moot Court Competition in Austin. We won and went on to the national finals in New York. It was quite a run.

Stuart and his wife, Linda Mitchell Price (the niece of longtime US senator George Mitchell), also received their law degrees from the University of Tulsa. Friends for many years, when TU wanted to raise three hundred thousand dollars to update and renovate the moot courtroom, we were all happy to help.

So just about thirty years after my big moot-court win on the TU campus, I was back for the ribbon cutting and formal dedication of the Price and Turpen Courtroom, remembering that the now-renovated room was where I began one of my major law-school achievements. As I looked around, I was warmed by the presence of many of my best friends—Stuart Price, of course, and Linda Mitchell Price, along with many others—including a great mentor I've told you about earlier, the noted criminal-defense attorney Pat Williams, as well my law partners, Tulsa civic leaders, and Tulsa University supporters George Kaiser, Ben Abney, Mike Case, and Mike Peyton. We were honored to have a video greeting from Senator George Mitchell and a keynote address from Judge Robert Henry.

Pat, in fact, brought back another, very different memory of moot court. I remembered arguing another moot-court case my second year in law school, which involved the insanity defense in a criminal case. Later on, when I was fresh out of law school and working as a legal intern for Pat, we had a case that involved a Tulsa County man named Clarence Durham. He was accused of murdering his wife and then trying to kill himself, and using the insanity defense, we got him off.

But that's not the end of the story. Some time later, when I was Muskogee County district attorney, I was walking down the street in Muskogee one day when a man approached me. "Remember me?" he asked.

Of course, I did. It was Clarence Durham.

He thanked me for his freedom and went on by. I didn't think much more about it until a Friday night a couple of years later when I got a call from my investigator.

"Boss," he said, "we've got a double homicide. A guy named Clarence Durham killed his wife. And then, when the police approached his house, he shot himself."

For me, that weekend phone call was eye-opening, although that doesn't begin to describe it. Let's just say it was the end of a certain amount of innocence, naïveté, and even idealism where I was concerned. I couldn't help thinking that had Clarence lived, the case would've come full circle for me. As district attorney, I had responsibility for prosecuting him. And yet years earlier, I had helped my mentor Pat Williams get him off with an insanity defense. And even earlier than that, in the University of Tulsa law school's moot courtroom, I argued for the insanity defense.

All of this and more went through my head as I stood watching the dedication ceremonies, with good friends all around me. Almost three decades ago, I left that building and campus to begin a life in law; now I was back, blessed with a resume that ranged from Oklahoma's attorney general to national political and legal activist and serious gubernatorial candidate to a partnership in one of the top law firms in the area—still striving every second, every minute, every day to make a difference as well as a living.

I had come full circle back to this place, from a fresh-faced student to a world- wise middle-aged man who'd done well enough to become a benefactor for his alma mater. I don't have to tell you how good it made me feel to have my name on a part of a place that held, and continues to hold, so much significance for me. You have the power to do the same.

TO SCAFFOLD RHETORIC

All the changes in the world, for good or evil,
were first brought about by words.

—Jacqueline Kennedy Onassis

As someone who's long been fascinated by the power
and meaning of words, I was particularly taken with
historian James C. Humes' book *Churchill* (Stein and
Day, 1980). Beginning with the famed John F. Kennedy
quote about Winston Churchill—"he mobilized the
English language and sent it into battle"—it reveals,
among other things, the existence of an unpublished
Churchill manuscript titled *The Scaffolding of Rhetoric.*

Humes wrote that Churchill's idea about how to
build an oration—to "scaffold rhetoric"—consisted
of four factors: the right words, a certain rhythm, the
mounting of an argument, and the use of analogy. But
after writing about those factors, Hume wrapped that
chapter up with one of the most powerful paragraphs
I've ever read, introducing it by explaining that "to

Churchill, the style of the orator is not nearly as important as his sincerity."

That's an enlightening phrase and a fitting introduction to the Churchill quote that closes the chapter:

> Before he can inspire them with any emotion, he must be swayed by it himself. When he would rouse their indignation, his heart is filled with anger. Before he can move their tears, his own must flow. To convince them he must himself believe. His opinions may change as their impressions fade, but every orator means what he says the moment he says it. He may be often inconsistent. He is never consciously insincere.

In many ways, this gets back to everything I've talked about in this book, to all the words I've used in these pages. It's about preparation in the courtroom and in life.

It's about the ability to get a jury or an audience bobbin' and noddin' in agreement. It's about "sales as a transference of belief," the bit of wisdom Harland Stonecipher gave me years ago. It all has to do with how deeply words *matter*—and how the *sincerity* behind those words matters the most. In my years of speaking to meetings of the National Association of Attorneys General all over the country, I'll bet I've quoted Churchill a thousand times: "He may be often inconsistent. He is *never* consciously insincere."

Ultimately, it really does all come down to that one word: sincerity.

In a 2003 speech to the Law Review Banquet of the Oklahoma City University School of Law, Oklahoma district court judge Nancy Coats gave a brief but memorable speech titled simply "The Power of Words." It's an enlightening and densely packed bit of oration that includes this observation: "A single well-chosen word can win a case, or a heart, or enforce a contract. A single ill-chosen word or comment can, on the other hand, breach a contract, destroy a relationship, or lose a case."

You never know what impact words—especially public ones—are going to have on those who hear them. But if you remember that one simple word, *sincerity*, it'll go a long way toward helping you make a positive impact.

I'm a great believer in axioms, as you can see from all my chapter headings. To me, they sum up in a few words some universal truths we should all ponder. I believe in every single one of them that you'll read here—and I mean that sincerely.

It's not at the head of a chapter, but another one I like is, "You must be laborious before you can be glorious." That's a line I've used in a lot of public-speaking engagements over the years, including a commencement speech to the 1983 class at Coweta High School. As I've said, you never know what, if any, effect your words are going to have at any given time, but that phrase and the rest of the speech hit home to at least a couple of members of that crowd. Almost twenty years later, in January of 2003, I received a three-page handwritten letter from Coweta's Vance Warren, who had been in the audience that evening. He told me how he'd related when I'd spoken about having humble beginnings, and working to advance myself.

"You were there that night," he wrote, "not just to speak, but to carry a message. That message you carried has helped me and my son for almost 20 years this May.

"My son," he continued, "was very impatient—as any young person is, I suppose. I wanted to work with him in that area, and I needed a 'working tool.' You gave me that tool as you told them, 'You must be laborious before you can be glorious,' and that, sir, was the tool I needed."

After they'd heard my speech, Mr. Warren suggested that his son, Marlin, consider a degree in criminal justice. And Marlin not only did that, but he earned a master's degree, worked successfully in juvenile justice for Tulsa County and, in 2002, was named Law Enforcement Officer of the Year for his work as a deputy sheriff in Tulsa.

"I recall many times when he called me from college discouraged and impatient," wrote Mr. Warren. "And each time I'd tell him, 'Now, son, remember what Mike Turpen said. 'You must be laborious before you can be glorious,' and that would do it."

He closed by asking me to share his letter with my children. I hope he doesn't mind that I shared parts of it with you as well. When I used the phrase that ultimately meant so much to Vance Warren and to his son, I was sincere. Above all, I meant what I said. And since we don't know what kind of an impact our words will have, don't we owe it to our listeners and ourselves to at least believe every one we utter?

Presenting my science fair project on rocket propulsion, Sam Houston Elementary School, Tulsa, OK, 1961.

Meeting with rocket scientist Dr. Wernher von Braun after winning the school science fair in 1961. Speaking about the "Space Race", Dr. von Braun told me that, "We have overcome gravity, but the paperwork is killing us."

WILL IT

> What is the most important thing a man needs
> if he wants to build? The will to do it.
>
> —Wernher von Braun

In the 1999 theatrical feature *October Sky*, well-known young actor Jake Gyllenhaal played a coal-miner's kid whose life changed forever in October of 1957, when Russia puts Sputnik, the first satellite, into orbit and the Space Race began. Based on the autobiographical book by Homer H. Hickam Jr., the film depicts a fired-up group of kids dubbed "rocket boys" eaten up with the romance of space and inspired by an inscribed picture young Hickam had received in the mail from the father of space travel, Wernher von Braun.

The scenes with the young rocketeers, sending their own lovingly constructed miniature missiles into the skies, were repeated for real in countless cities and towns all across the country, as youthful imaginations opened up—and an earnest rivalry with the USSR began—following the launch of Sputnik

1. In north Tulsa, my friend Gordo Ewing and I were two of the kids who caught the space fever; by the late fifties, we were rocket boys ourselves, writing to space-related military bases for photos of rockets and astronauts, launching our handcrafted creations with a variety of experimental propulsive (our fuel tanks, as Gordo recently recalled in an email, were made out of steak-sauce cans), and educating ourselves on current technologies as best we could. After we found out that the big boys in America's space program used liquefied oxygen in their rockets, we both went on a quest to get some of that stuff, realizing that our solid-fuel craft—dubbed T/E Success by its creators, Turpen and Ewing—was kids' stuff compared to America's *serious* liquid-fuel rocketry. I remember bugging people out at Douglas Aircraft, who'd always answer in the same way, "Are you kidding? We can't give you liquid oxygen!"

Meanwhile, Gordo and I kept at it, and in 1961, I won first place in the Houston Elementary School's science fair with my project on rocket propulsion. In that way, I was a lot like the kid Homer Hickam in *October Sky*, who also became a science-fair champion, thanks in part to a female public-school teacher who encouraged him to pursue his otherworldly dreams. His was a Miss Riley (played in the movie by Laura Dern). Mine was Ms. Arlene Hinckley, a science teacher at good old Houston Elementary.

The youthful Hickam and I also shared a hero— as did virtually every rocket kid at the time—in von Braun, the former German scientist who'd been living in Huntsville, Alabama, since 1950, directing the

Marshall Space Flight Center and working on missile and rocket development. (I had two major heroes at the time; the second one had a space worthy nickname: Mickey Mantle, the "Commerce Comet.")

But I did Hickam one better. While he had a signed picture of von Braun, sent in response to a mailed question, I actually got to meet and talk with the man himself.

It all came about because of my proud mother, Marge, and the enterprising Ms. Hinckley, who found out that von Braun was going to be visiting Tulsa and arranged for our meeting. When it came to her kids, Mom left little to chance—the photo of young science-fair-winner Mike Turpen with the great rocket scientist von Braun, which remains a family heirloom, was taken by James Abbott, her childhood friend from their days at Whittier Elementary School in Tulsa.

Of course, I don't need Mr. Abbott's wonderful black-and-white photograph to recall that memorable meeting. All I have to do is close my eyes for a moment, and I can recall it all as though it just happened—my sixth grade self, dressed in a pair of my brother's pants that were too big for me, walking down the staircase at KVOO Channel 2. It was my first time in a television studio, which was daunting enough. But even more important, I was going to meet the man who helped lead me into my love of space and rocketry. Von Braun was in town for a symposium arranged by then senator Robert S. Kerr and sponsored by the National Aeronautics and Space Administration and the Tulsa Chamber of Commerce. Bringing in experts from all around the country to speak and appear on panels, it was dubbed the First National Conference on Peaceful Uses of Space. Dr. Wernher von Braun was speaking on launch-vehicle programs.

But at this moment, he was in the TV studio speaking to me.

Many of us have had the chance to meet our heroes, and sometimes it just doesn't work out as well as you'd like. There's a cliché about how heroes sometimes have feet of clay, and that's true. They can turn out to be people you probably wouldn't like very much if you knew them.

On the other hand, instead of feet of clay, they can have the wings of angels—and that's the way it was with von Braun. He was very fatherly. Very reassuring. Very warm. I was amazed that he wanted to spend any time talking to me because, even then, I knew that he was very important, and I was just a little guy who'd won a local science fair.

I still remember some of the conversation almost verbatim.

"Well, are you into rocketry?" he asked me after we'd been introduced.

"Yes, sir," I replied, "and I'm also into baseball."

"Did you ever hit a baseball through a neighbor's window?"

"I sure have."

"Well," he said, "guess what? I shot some rockets through *my* neighbor's window."

I just loved that. He was *relating* to me. Here's the guy who inspired me to get into rocketry, to study the methods of propulsion that led to my science-fair exhibit, and he's talking about how my baseball through a window and his rocket through a window are pretty much the same thing.

I also remember asking him about the space program, and his response: "Well, we've overcome gravity, young man, but the paperwork is killing us."

I've come to see that as a metaphor about how greatness can be pulled down by the mundane. Here was a man trying to put our satellites into orbit, working to put a man on the moon before the Russians, and the triplicate copies and long hallways, the government bureaucracy, was taking big chunks of time and energy that would be better put in other places.

Finally, Wernher von Braun told me to aim for the stars—and the fact that it was coming from a man who truly aimed all he had in that direction gave the statement special importance in my young mind. He signed a copy of the conference booklet for me—I still have it—and then our meeting was over.

Of course, I left his side an inspired young man, wanting to work with America's space program more than ever. In the subsequent years, however, I learned that to be a rocket scientist, you had to be a *rocket scientist*. The *October Sky* protagonist, Homer Hickam, really *did* grow up to become a NASA scientist. But I had to finally conclude that whatever talents I have lay in other areas. Still, Wernher von Braun, a famous scientist who found some time for a little rocket-obsessed boy nearly half a century ago, remains an inspiration. And along with his observation about the paperwork killing him, the von Braun quote that begins this chapter also has a special meaning for me. The importance of having the will to do something has long been a guiding principle of my own life. It was practical and inspirational advice for the heady days of the Space Age. And it still is.

FORGIVE YOUR
ADVERSARIES

Forgiveness, not blame.

You've probably heard of that alleged ancient Chinese curse that goes, "May you live in interesting times." Well, in 1986, the race for the Democratic nomination for Oklahoma's governor was nothing if not interesting, and I was right in the middle of it. The field included such characters as Billy Joe Clegg, who'd come to the debates with a beaker and say, "All right now, everybody pee in the cup and let's see who's on drugs." Also in the running was a businessman named David Walters, who ultimately became the nominee, following the primary election and then a runoff against the primary's other top vote getter—which was me.

I was the state's attorney general then, and I still believe that at that moment in the state's history—and in my own personal and political history—I was the best person for the job. I would've brought a whole new team of people in, and it would've been my opportunity to impact Oklahoma in a meaningful way and help make the state a better place to live. I was deprived of that opportunity, something that was especially hard to take because, going in, I was considered the frontrunner for the nomination.

But David Walters beat me. In part, it was because he called me a career politician. That was about the only ammo he had, but it worked, even though I tried to diffuse the attack by humorously answering, "Well, I want to be, but I'm not yet. I just got here."

He had the best consulting team in the whole country back then—David Doak and Bob Shrum out of Washington, DC—and they kept hammering away at me in their ads. "Record farm failures! Record bank failures! Record bankruptcies! Blame it on the attorney general!" Now, of course, I had nothing to do with any of that, but beyond my crack on the "career politician" tag, I didn't defend myself. I never responded. I took the high road in the primary because I was the frontrunner. I had the name recognition. I was going to win.

But he came out of nowhere and beat me in the primary by saying he was the businessman and I was the career politician.

That race taught me a lot about politics, and one of the things it taught me is that you've got to respond to negative campaigning. Whatever they say about you, no matter how outrageous or wrong it is, you've got to respond *immediately*. Otherwise, it's a tacit admission of guilt. Don't you imagine that John Kerry would like to roll back the clock to early 2004 so he could immediately respond to the relentless swift-boat ads that helped torpedo his run for president of the United States?

After coming in second in the primary, I regrouped for the runoff election and, with the invaluable aid of friends and supporters, came so close to winning that there was serious talk of a recount. David Walters went on to run against a beloved and resurgent Republican, Henry Bellmon, who'd become the state's first Republican governor in 1963. He beat Walters in the general election, becoming governor for a second stretch.

I did not rally behind Walters. As the runner-up for the nomination, I didn't give him any help against Bellmon, and at the risk of sounding immodest, I'm sure that was one of the factors in Bellmon's win. The truth is, though, I think it was Bellmon's time once again. I don't think *I* would've beaten him if I'd been the Democratic nominee instead of David. I have a lot of regard and respect for Henry Bellmon, and Walters ran a pretty good race against him, almost coming out on top, but in retrospect, I'm glad I wasn't put in the position of trying to beat him myself.

Four years later, in 1990, Walters ran again. Frankly, I was still mad about some of the tactics he'd used against me in '86, mad that he'd stolen my dream, and my guy in that Democratic primary was seven-time congressman Wes Watkins. But Walters beats Watkins and State House Speaker Steve Lewis, and all of a sudden it's Democrat David Walters running against Republican Bill Price, a former US attorney.

Both of them called and asked for my help. And while I liked and respected Bill Price—and still do—I had to tell him I was going to help Walters.

Price couldn't believe it, of course. He reminded me of the campaign David had run against me four years ago. But I'd made up my mind, and a month before the general election, I ended up defending David Walters in a critical scenario that I believe helped him become governor.

To state it as simply as possible, during the campaigning, Walters claimed that Price had been fined on a working interest he had in an oil well. And right down the stretch of the governor's race, Price sued Walters for defamation of character. In addition to suing him, Price was demanding an apology, a retraction, all that. So Walters assembled a group of people at his home, and he asked me to be there.

There was another lawyer present, a man justifiably well known to members of the profession in this state and beyond, and he told Walters, "I think they may have a legitimate case against you, and I think you should apologize. Right now."

"Well," returned Walters, "I had a slightly different tactic in mind than conceding that his lawsuit has merit and apologizing."

"I think you overstepped the bounds when you said he was fined," the lawyer continued. "Wells have all these working interests, and royalty-interest owners, and technically, he wasn't fined."

Then I piped up. "David," I said, "only a lawyer would think about filing a lawsuit in the middle of an election and try to win at the jury box instead of the ballot box. I think you've got to fight him all the way." The lawyer was thinking like a lawyer, you see, while I was thinking more as a politician, a tactician.

So the next day, three of us lawyers were scheduled to appear at a press conference on behalf of Walters. One of them was the man who'd given Walters the advice to apologize. The other was Andy Coats, the recent mayor of Oklahoma City and also a noted legal figure. The conference was to be at the state capitol, and we were all in a room deciding what we were going to say when Andy Coats got a call.

After he hung up, he told us, "That was my law firm, and they tell me it would be a conflict of interest for me to go down there." Not long afterward, the other lawyer got a call, and afterward, he said, "I just found out I used to represent somebody that's involved in this case, so I can't be there either."

So then there was one. Me.

I went to the press conference by myself, and there I stated that we believed Price's lawsuit to be frivolous and repeated publicly what I'd said at Walter's house the night before—that I thought only a lawyer would try to win an election at the jury box instead of the ballot box.

Just about a month later, Walters won the election, becoming Oklahoma's twenty-fourth governor.

That, however, wasn't the end of Price's lawsuit. Bill pushed it all the way. After I argued the case in Oklahoma County District Court and won a motion for summary judgment, getting it kicked out of court,

Bill Price took it all the way to the Oklahoma Supreme Court. It was resolved many years later, long after David Walters's term as governor, when those justices voted 5–4 to affirm the motion for summary judgment I'd made years before.

David beat me for the Democratic nomination for governor in 1986. In 1990, he needed my help, and I got over my bitterness and forgave him for what I felt he'd done against me and moved on. I'm not going to tell you it was easy. But after I lost to him, I realized that nobody wanted to hear me talk about all the things that had gone wrong, so I started using the line "Forgive and remember." I meant that I was going to try to forgive everybody and move on, turn the page and write a new chapter. At the same time, I knew I'd be a chump if I didn't remember exactly what had happened—what had gone right and what had gone wrong, who'd stayed hitched to you and who hadn't. That's what I meant by "Forgive and remember."

I still believe that. But I think the variant on that statement that appears at the top of this chapter is even better. I should add that the idea of "Forgiveness, not blame" also came to me because of my association with David Walters.

After he was elected governor, David made me one of his advisors. Before he made a judicial appointment, he'd call me. Then I became the chairman of the state's Democratic Party, which led to my becoming the chairman of Oklahoma's campaign for Bill Clinton. After losing the governor's race in '86, I married Susan, the woman of my dreams, and we started a family. I began to help build a law firm. And after David's election in 1990, I became and remained one of his advisors.

Then around Christmas of 1991, a little over a year into the Walters' administration, David's son Shaun took his own life. He was in a coma at Baptist Hospital in Oklahoma City, and David called me and said, "They've told us we need to try to wake him up. Would you come over and talk to, or read to, my son?"

He never came out of the coma. But while I was there, my pastor, Mike Anderson, came in, just as a friend, and he told David, simply, "Forgiveness, not blame. Forgiveness."

I'll never forget it. Mike said, "David, you have to forgive your son for doing this. You've got to forgive all the people you think have brought your son to this point. Christ said on the cross, 'Forgiveness, not blame.' Forgive your son. Forgive all the people who have tormented you. Forgive your detractors. Forgive."

Forgiveness is difficult, no mistake. But I think one of the strongest lessons in life is that you just can't talk theoretically about it.

You can't leave forgiveness in the pew after church is out. You must apply it to your life. This life lesson was brought home so beautifully in such a tragic situation by Pastor Mike Anderson.

I have remained friends with the man who beat me for the Democratic nomination more than two decades ago. Just recently, in fact, McGuinness High School in Oklahoma City, where the Walters kids all went, was in the midst of a capital campaign, and that gave me an idea. I approached David and his wife, Rhonda, with the idea that we raise some money and do something for the school in Shaun's name. Through the efforts and contributions of many people, we raised more than two hundred thousand dollars, which will fund in full the school's new Shaun Walters Memorial Reception Area.

For the Walters family, as well as for me, it will be a monument of forgiveness, not blame.

CHOOSE YOUR BATTLES

Don't dance every dance.

—Henry Bellmon

One of the pieces of wisdom I always try to pass on to aspiring politicians is something Henry Bellmon, Oklahoma's first Republican governor and a towering figure in our state's political history, told me: "Don't dance every dance."

What it means essentially is you have to pick and choose your battles—especially if you're holding a public office. That may not sound particularly profound, but I believe it's one of the most important bits of advice a politician can take. In fact, I believe if I'd heeded Bellmon's words, I might have become the Democratic nominee for Oklahoma governor in 1986, instead of *nearly* becoming the nominee. (Ironically enough, I would've been running against Bellmon himself in the general election.)

Instead, against my own intuition and better judgment, I danced a dance that I should have sat out.

When I was Oklahoma attorney general, the state retirement board came to me and asked for an opinion. An Oklahoman-affirmed attorney-general opinion is the law until, or unless, it is overturned by one of the states' high courts. Now the only time an attorney general's opinion gets solicited is when a government entity is dealing with a controversial or divisive issue, and that was the case here. The question was whether or not Oklahoma judges could count their years of service in the military toward their state retirement. As is the case with most government employees, the age that a judge can retire and start drawing a pension is influenced by how many years he or she has been a part of the system. I was being asked whether or not the years of military service, if any, served by the judges could be added when retirement eligibility was calculated.

Tom Cornish, who's currently a bankruptcy judge down in Okmulgee, represented the judges, and he came to me and said, "Mike, this is clear. Look at all this law. It indicates that you *can* count military-service time toward your retirement. You're not going to take *that* away from them, are you? I mean, they were serving their country."

But a lawyer on my staff, an assistant attorney general and a young man whose opinion I valued and respected, saw it the other way. He thought my ruling should go against the judges.

So Tom Cornish came in representing Oklahoma's judges and showed me a good argument, but my own staff member researched it thoroughly and gave me an opposite opinion. Those in the legal profession know that there's case law that goes either way on almost every issue you can imagine—the law is legal instead of logical—so both opinions had some validity.

Ultimately, I stuck with my lawyer and issued a ruling saying that Oklahoma judges couldn't take those years. And immediately, I was branded as a foe of veterans.

Every county courthouse I'd visit—and I visited a *lot* of them while I was attorney general—the judges would ask a variation of the same question: "Mike, are you against veterans?"

"No," I'd say. "I was just asked to give an opinion. I didn't even want to give it."

"Well, you could have gone the other way."

"But my lawyer said…"

"Yeah, but *you're* the attorney general. You didn't have to answer the opinion. You get asked a lot of things you don't answer, and a lot of other things you take a long time to answer, and besides, you could let the courts decide something like this. You didn't have to do it yourself."

Of course, they were right. I didn't have to dance that dance, but I did. I had a talented young assistant AG who looked at the law and believed he got it right, and I went with his opinion rather than with my own political judgment. He wasn't elected to his position by the people. I was. I stood up, but what did I stand up *for?*

Did I mention I was running for governor while all this was going on?

No one running for office wants to be seen as being against America's fighting men and women, but because I'd stuck with my guy, my staffer, and issued an attorney general's opinion on what amounted to an obscure legal issue, I was being tarred with the anti-veteran brush. I have no doubt that this perception hurt me with voters, perhaps enough to be the deciding factor in my loss of the Democratic gubernatorial primary to David Walters.

On top of everything else, I was wrong. How do I know? Because later on, the Oklahoma Supreme Court overruled the opinion I'd issued. Of course, everyone on the Supreme Court is a judge—but still, based on their interpretation of my opinion, I was wrong.

In the meantime, I took a huge political hit for being, quote, "anti-veteran." Stepping onto the floor for a dance I didn't have to take, I made a wrong step, and it hurt me and my career.

Since then, I've been honored to speak to AG's offices all over the country, talking to hundreds of attorneys general and their staffers. It's something I enjoy doing. My advice always includes Bellmon's deceptively simple-sounding advice. Sure enough, you don't have to dance every dance. In fact, you'll be a lot better off if every once in awhile, you just sit one out.

END-ZONE MIRACLES

It ain't over 'til it's over.

—Yogi Berra

People who know me may be shocked to hear me say I'm obsessive about something. But I am. It's sports, and I believe that's my only real obsession. My collection of sports memorabilia includes the very first issue of *Sports Illustrated* from August 16, 1953, with a cover showing one of my all-time baseball heroes, Milwaukee Braves slugger Eddie Mathews, teeing off on a pitch as a stadium full of fans look on. Given to me by my mother many years ago, it's one of my prized possessions.

I also love great writing about sports. There seems to be something about baseball, especially, that draws wonderful words out of writers. Maybe it's because baseball and childhood are so inextricably tied together, and as our heroes grow old and pass on, we feel our own inescapable mortality—the death of our youth—through them.

When Mickey Mantle died, commentator, comedian, and fellow Oklahoman Argus Hamilton wrote that Mantle "represented the possibilities and dreams of childhood…[remaining] the signifier of our youth as long as he lived."

When Roger Maris, Mantle's fabled home-run partner on those legendary sixties Yankee teams, passed, newspaperman Art Spander wrote these haunting words: "The boys of summer turn quickly into the men of autumn. One day we read their stats. The next, we read their obits."

While there are exceptions—what man can hear a dying Lou Gehrig call himself "the luckiest man on the face of the earth" without getting a catch in his throat?—most of the memorable lines are not written and uttered by the players themselves. Perhaps they're too busy just playing the game.

The great New York Yankee catcher and outfielder Yogi Berra, a valuable teammate of Mantle and Maris, is an exception. Yogi has become famous not only for his play on the field, but also for fractured pronouncements, like "Baseball is 90 percent mental—the other half is physical," "It's so crowded nobody goes there anymore," and "I really didn't say everything I said." Among those "Yogisms" is the epigraph of this chapter, which, like most of Berra's oft-quoted words of wisdom, contains more than a nugget of truth.

Certainly, "It ain't over 'til is over" applies beautifully to other sports, including high-school football. It's especially applicable to the game played between the Owasso Rams and Jenks Trojans in Jenks, Oklahoma, on November 16, 1974. I convinced one of my great mentors, Pat Williams, to accompany me that evening, by explaining the power of the rivalry between Jenks and Owasso. During this particular season, the ante had been upped because the Rams were playing the powerhouse Trojans in the Class 6A semifinals, after already having lost once to Jenks during the regular season.

In addition, Rams head coach Gary Harper and a lot of his staff—including assistant coach Rick Rogers—played football at Jenks. Rogers's dad, Red Rogers, built a mighty reputation as the Trojans head coach. So on this night, father and son would be facing off against one another, adding an extra layer to the long-lived rivalry.

I had a family-oriented interest in the game myself. My little brother, Frosty, was playing for the Rams that night.

Then, as now, Jenks was the team to beat in Class 6A. For the majority of the game, the Rams were doing just that. But with less than a minute left in the last quarter, the Jenks quarterback connected with his receiver on a touchdown pass, putting the Trojans ahead, 14–10. After a kickoff and three option plays, we were on the Jenks' twenty-nine-yard line, with only a couple of seconds left for an all-or-nothing play.

What happened next was simply the greatest play in Owasso football history. That's what *Tulsa World* sportswriter Mike Brown called it in a 1993 column, and certainly, no one who was in the stands that night would dispute that title.

Quarterback Stacey Lamb got the ball and rolled right, but his primary receiver was covered. So with the Trojan defense in hard pursuit, he doubled back, rolled to his left, and spied my brother open in the end zone. As Lamb let go of the pass, the clock went off, signaling the end of the game. Of course, since the play was already going when the clock stopped, it was still a live play.

Frosty caught Lamb's long, desperate heave, and Owasso won, 16–14, against a very tough opponent in its home stadium. The folks on the Owasso side of the field, including me, erupted. A few seconds before, victory had seemed impossible and a lot of Rams fans had already packed it in and headed for the parking lot, hoping at least to beat the traffic.

On this wondrous, unbelievable night, however, the impossible happened. The 1974 6A Oklahoma high-school semifinals truly weren't over until they were over.

The Rams would go on to take it all, becoming state champions. A decade or so later, Lamb was elected mayor of Owasso, and Frosty, by then a successful businessman, was elected to the town's school board. So in a sense, it really wasn't over, even for those two, when the ball game ended. They swapped their football uniforms for business suits and continued to do positive things for their town and its people.

FORGOTTEN MIDDLE CLASS

A word to the wise is efficient.

I know that I've changed the end of that famous quote, which in Latin is *Verbum sapineti satis ost*, or "A word to the wise is *sufficient*." (The great American humorist James Thurber also modified it to "A word to the wise isn't sufficient if it doesn't make sense.") But in the case of Bill Clinton, a few words I shared during his first term were an efficient reminder of how important it was to get back to basics.

The first time Bill Clinton took a run at the presidency, his theme was "Fighting for the forgotten middle class." Early in his campaign, he visited Oklahoma City. Riding from the airport to the state capitol, I asked him, "Well, what do you think of your chances?"

"I can't *believe* Sam Nunn dropped out," he replied. "I can't *believe* Mario Cuomo's not going to run. Everybody's dropping out. I mean, honestly, I got into this thing for VP or whatever, but now it looks like we may run the table!"

At the time, Clinton was handing out a brochure. It was fairly crude, like something you'd see in a local race. Remember, this was very early in his national political career, even before James Carville had become his lead strategist. In fact, Hillary and Bill created the brochure together, coming up with the "Fighting for the forgotten middle class" slogan.

That theme resonated with the American people. For that reason, and many others, Bill Clinton was sworn in as America's forty-second president. Only a couple of years later, Newt Gingrich and newly empowered legislators buoyed by the so-called Republican Revolution were determined to thwart his agenda, if not actually bring down the president of the United States.

As Oklahoma chair of the Clinton-Gore campaign, I was summoned to the White House, along with other Clinton supporters from across the country in late 1994. It was the holiday season, and there was a party that night. But first we gathered for a meeting run by White House chief of staff Leon Panetta.

Sitting in the back of the room, I was one of the first to speak. I asked Panetta if I could give a message to the president. He agreed, and so I began.

"You need to get back to where you started—back to basics." I brought a copy of Clinton's old brochure, the one about fighting for the middle class, and held it up so that everyone in the room could see it.

"Mr. President," I continued, "you need to fight for the forgotten middle class. We may *need* condoms in the schools. And we can talk all day about gays in the military. I believe we're on the right side of that issue. But for God's sake, let's get back to the forgotten middle class, the working men and women of this country! They need some help! That's the platform we *ran* on!"

I said my piece in an impassioned way, and the meeting went on. I hoped that I'd made my point sufficiently enough that Panetta would pass it to the president.

That night at the party, I found myself in the receiving line with the Clintons, and one of them said, "We heard that you pretty much took over the meeting today."

"Well," I returned, "not exactly. I showed one of your old brochures."

"Do you still have it with you?"

"Sure." I dug it out of my pocket and handed it over to the president. He looked at it and then looked at his wife with a smile.

"Hillary, remember this?" he asked, holding it so she could see it. "It's the one you and I made together."

I'm not kidding. That's exactly what he said. Turns out it was their first brochure. They'd collaborated on it when he'd first started running, before Carville came along to mastermind the campaign.

"That was where you started, Mr. President," I told him, "and that's what you've got to get back to. I know where you are on all those other issues, and I'm with you, brother. But politically, with Gingrich and all of 'em coming at you, you've got to get back to the forgotten middle class."

Part of the reason this may have been on my mind was something I'd heard on Tulsa radio station KRMG a few days earlier. Someone phoned their morning announcer, John Erling, and said, "The Democratic Party used to be the party of the working people, and now it's the party of the nonworking people."

Of course, those nonworking people need representation too, but the perception—encouraged by the Republicans—was that all Democrats, including the president, didn't care about hardworking Americans any more.

The president looked at the brochure a few moments more, and then he asked, "May I keep this?"

"Sure," I said, and I moved on down the line.

After I'd been home for a few days, I received a letter from the president.

"Mike," he wrote, "it was great to see you at last week's holiday party. That old campaign brochure really brought back a lot of memories. Also, I think it put some perspective on what lies ahead. Mike, we must restore the rights of the forgotten middle class."

Not long after that, in a speech given on December 19, 1994, he outlined a new plan for a four-point plan he called the middle-class bill of rights, which he said would "help a new generation of hardworking people get the right education and skills, raise their children, and keep their families strong so that they can get ahead in the new American economy."

That was a Forrest Gump moment for me because a few words helped put the United States back on track—efficiently. He eventually sent the "forgotten middle class" brochure back to me. It's framed in my office.

Susan and me at a White House Christmas Party, December 1994, with President Bill Clinton and First Lady Hillary Clinton.

MEET THE FINISH LINE

Just have a good attitude and trust God, and
everything will be okay.

—Ford Price

You'll recall that I offered my son Patrick and six of
his friends a hundred dollars each a few years ago—
if they'd memorize Rudyard Kipling's poem. They all
took me up on the challenge. While the one hundred
dollars enriched their billfolds, the poem enriched their
thoughts and perceptions, as I knew it would.

I also mentioned how the poem helped poetry club
member David Price deal with a terrible bout of spinal
meningitis, which he contracted in the fall of 2006. A
year and a half later, his cousin—another poetry club
member in full standing—was diagnosed with his own
severe illness. In April of 2008, Ford Price III, then a
senior at Heritage Hall in Oklahoma City, found out
he had a rare kind of cancer known as Ewing's sarcoma.

It seems amazing to me that out of only a half
dozen or so young men in the poetry group, two of

them—cousins, to boot—would have to wage battles against life- threatening sicknesses. But they're both tough kids, and their courage has been nothing short of inspirational.

In July of 2008, Ford was operated on in Boston. A tumor the size of a softball was removed from his hip. The doctors had to cut out part of his right iliac bone.

Then came the arduous, soul-crushing months of chemotherapy, bone scans, biopsies, and other cancer-related tests, many of them painful and protracted. Ford took the chemo fluids, which he dubbed Orange Gatorade, and other treatment back home, at the Jimmy Everest Center for Cancer and Blood Disorders in the OU Children's Hospital. Ironically, a couple of years earlier, he had been one of the organizers and participants in a charity dodgeball tournament to raise funds for the center.

At every step, Ford not only had his own remarkable courage and faith to rely on. He also had the unwavering support of his parents, friends, and classmates, who linked together to make a strong, resilient safety net that surrounded him during his ordeal.

After his diagnosis, University of Oklahoma coach Bob Stoops—who'd met with the poetry club in April, the same month Ford was diagnosed with cancer—sent him an encouraging note and an autographed football, which immediately became one of Ford's most prized possessions. Then, when Ford traveled to Boston for his surgery, star New England Patriots receiver Wes Welker took him on a tour of the team's facilities, visited him in the hospital, and gifted him with pictures and an autographed helmet. (Welker had played at Ford's high school, Heritage Hall, before going on to Texas Tech and then the NFL.)

Ford, who's played football and basketball since he was very small, was projected to be a starting linebacker for Oklahoma City's Heritage Hall Chargers. All of that changed when he received the diagnosis, of course, but he was still a big part of the 2008 team effort, getting out to cheer on his comrades whenever he was able. The Chargers, including his fellow poetry-club member and All-State quarterback Turner Peterson, voted to dedicate their season to him. They all wore armbands with the number 43, Ford's jersey number. The armbands were also worn by footballers from two other Oklahoma City schools, McGuinness and Casady, where Ford had many friends.

Meanwhile, students from those three schools began making "love buckets" for Ford, containers holding everything from candy to personal messages and a Bible. His aunt delivered them to him while he was in the hospital.

Many of us—including, quietly, Bob Stoops—visited Ford through his months of illness, relying always on the deeply spiritual and hopeful emails from his mother that kept us informed of just exactly what her son was going through.

In a story about Ford that appeared in the fall 2008 issue of the *Westminster School Alumni Retrospective*, he's quoted as saying, "No matter how difficult the situation, attitude is everything." Over months of treatment, that philosophy was tested again and again, but Ford held it together, keeping up the good attitude, sometimes to the amazement of friends and family who were looking on.

In that same story, I'm proud to say that Ford talks about some of the advice he received as a member of the poetry club. You've already seen it in this book: ES, EM, ED—every second, every minute, every day. If that challenge to live life to the fullest, regardless of the circumstances, gave him any comfort or inspiration, then I'm happy to have shared it with him.

Of course, I saw myself as a mentor for Ford and the other boys. But I found, as I witnessed Ford struggling through his treatments and always doing his best to stay positive, that the mentor could become the mentored. I've drawn great strength from seeing his courage. As the axiom goes, courage is contagious, and his certainly was—not only for me, but for his family, friends, and teammates as well.

On December 23, 2008, Ford Price III was declared cancer-free. As tradition dictates, he rang a bell at the Jimmy Everest Center, and they put his picture on the wall. It was the happy ending to an incredible story of courage and determination and a testament to the power of prayer, the power of medicine, and the power of positive thinking.

A few weeks before that, on the day after Ford received his last chemotherapy treatment, the Heritage Hall Chargers had gone 15–0 and won the state championship. Their motto—and Ford's—was one simple word: finish.

And indeed, they both did.

POOR JUD IS DAID

Bring your flowers to the living.

When there's a profusion of flowers left over after a funeral, the natural impulse for many is to donate them to hospitals or nursing homes, with the thought that the blooms and blossoms will add a bit of cheer to the institutional surroundings and therefore do something to help someone else. It's a noble impulse, but what many hospital and nursing-home staff members will tell you is that funeral flowers aren't a good idea for their occupants because they too often remind people of death and dying.

I think that helps illustrate my belief that flowers should be for the living. In other words, you shouldn't wait until people are gone before expressing how much you care about them.

This whole philosophy was brought home to me recently by something that happened to my older brother, Brent.

You've read elsewhere in this book about my younger brother, Frosty, the man on the end of the pass termed as the greatest play in Owasso High School football history and the University of Tulsa relief pitcher who overcame an incredible illness to become a multimillionaire businessman. Now it's time to talk about the oldest of the Turpen boys, the Rev. Brent Turpen, who's a preacher at the Cumberland Presbyterian Church. He currently lives and works in Bowling Green, Kentucky, with his wife Mary Lou and two children John and Julie.

Not long ago, Brent was diagnosed with a tumor in his lower intestine. Surgery was quickly scheduled, and after the doctors removed it, they found out it was indeed malignant. But they're pretty sure they got it all, and at this writing, he hasn't had to have any chemotherapy or radiation treatments.

When we found out about the tumor, I started calling him a lot, trying to preach my own little philosophy to him, telling him to hang in there, that he was doing well and everything was going to be all right. And then at about noon on the day of his surgery, I called his hospital room to see if I could find out how he'd come through.

Imagine my surprise when I got Brent himself. And not only that, but he was pumped up and almost joyous.

"Hey, Mike," he greeted me, "how are you doing?"

I was momentarily confused. "My god! You're out of surgery?"

"Oh no, no," Brent said, "I'm getting ready to go *into* surgery."

He was supposed to undergo the knife that morning, but something had happened to push it back. If that was the case, I couldn't understand why my brother was so upbeat. After all, he was probably minutes away from a very serious operation.

"You sound good," I said.

"Mike," he returned, "I've got six preachers in here with me. *Six preachers*. They're from all over this city, and they're here praying over me, and I'm ready to go for my surgery."

Not long after that, he was wheeled into surgery, and he had the operation and recovered. Later on, Mary Lou told me that the single greatest moment in his life may have been that time right before he left his hospital room.

"What do you mean?" I asked her.

She said, "When those six preachers came in and prayed with him, he saw how much people cared about him."

That really spoke to me, partly because my daughter had just appeared in a production of the great musical *Oklahoma!* and the play was still very fresh in my mind. What Brent's wife said made me think of the scene in which Curly sings the famous "Poor Jud Is Daid" to the still-living Jud Frye. Throughout the song, Curly is essentially saying to Jud, "Visualize your own funeral. You've got to *die* before you find out how many people like you."

And now here was my brother—possibly facing death himself and certainly facing serious surgery. It would have been an uncertain and frightening thing for anybody, but because six of his peers from across Bowling Green gathered to show him that they cared, he was happy.

That's just an example of what I group under the heading of "Flowers for the Living." Those preachers didn't wait until after the surgery to show Brent that they were concerned about him. They came in and, by their presence, let him know how they felt about him *now* on this earth.

We all need to do more of that. People always need to know that we care about them, right here and right now. It's very important that we always try to deliver our flowers—whether actual or metaphorical—to the living, instead of waiting until it's too late.

BATTLES WORTH FIGHTING

Life's most persistent and urgent question is,
"What are you doing for others?"

—Martin Luther King Jr.

I'm proud to say that the late US representative Mike
Synar was my friend. And he was a fighter, tirelessly
taking on heavyweight special-interest groups when he
believed they were working against the best interests
of the people. He was a pit bull, for instance, in his
efforts to expose the tobacco industry for knowingly
misleading the American people and their government
about the addictiveness and damaging health effects of
its products.

For Mike, the catalyst for his battle with tobacco
was a personal one. In Talihina, Oklahoma, one of
the towns in Mike's district, a top high school athlete
named Sean Marsee had contracted oral cancer. An
outstanding runner with twenty-eight medals in track,
Sean had been dipping snuff since the age of twelve,
mistakenly believing—despite the warnings of his

mother, a registered nurse—that smokeless tobacco couldn't hurt him the way cigarettes could. By the time he was diagnosed with cancer, he was up to almost five tins of snuff a week.

Despite three harrowing operations, the cancer spread throughout his oral cavity, and he died less than a year after his high school graduation, craving snuff until the very end. It was Sean's terrifying and tragic story that provided the emotional courage for the most important political battle of Mike Synar's life—his David-versus-Goliath struggle against the leaders of the tobacco industry on the floor of Congress.

Mike began his passionate fight against big tobacco in the early eighties. I didn't get involved in that battle until later, when the law firm of Riggs, Abney, Neal, Turpen, Orbison, & Lewis—my "Band of Brothers"—joined Oklahoma attorney general Drew Edmondson in suing the tobacco industry.

Like my friend Mike Synar, I had a personal reason for joining the fight. Recently, my mother sent me a poem she'd found while cleaning out her house; I'd written it for my dad on one of his birthdays. The misspellings and juvenile passages indicate that I was very young when I composed it, which probably accounts for the fact that I didn't remember much about it when she gave it to me. But when I reread it after all the intervening years, a couple of lines jumped out at me. Along with the verses praising and kidding dad, I had written:

> You're still smoking three packs a day and you
> just keep throwing your money away.

Ken Turpen *was* a three-pack-a-day smoker for many years until he died of lung cancer at age fifty-three. And even at the very end, when the tobacco-induced disease had reduced his voice to a raspy whisper and he was in Tulsa Regional, where he lay dying, he'd call me aside and say, almost begging, "Mike. Please. Bring me some cigarettes. Bring me some Pall Malls."

Years went on, and others—including then president Bill Clinton—carried on the fight against the powerful tobacco companies. And then in 1996, Oklahoma attorney general Drew Edmondson filed a suit against the industry. The effort had begun with Mississippi's attorney general and Oklahoma became the fourteenth state to get on board.

It looked like a losing proposition from the beginning. In fifty years of litigation, the tobacco industry had never lost a case. It had the biggest law firms in the world behind it. But Edmondson and the other attorneys general across the country had a lot of the crusader in them too.

Of course, they needed help from private law firms, and that's where we came in, the group I call the Band of Brothers. Like the band of brothers in Shakespeare's *Henry V*, we at Riggs, Abney, Neal, Turpen, Orbison & Lewis go to battle together, fighting side by side, sometimes taking on opponents that make us look overmatched, but maintaining our loyalty and dedication to one another, our shared ideals, and the people we represent.

I joined the firm in 1986, after my unsuccessful run for Oklahoma governor. At the time, there were about seventeen lawyers there. Now with well over one hundred, Riggs, Abney, Neal, Turpen, Orbison & Lewis is one of the biggest and most successful, law firms in the state.

My good friend and law partner David Riggs and I brought the case against tobacco to the firm, and most observers believed we'd have no chance to win. The tobacco industry had a perfect half-century record of beating lawsuits and it continued to employ the best attorneys money could buy. We were told that the case was too big, that we would be better off not getting involved. Plus, it was a contingency case, so we wouldn't get paid a dime unless got a favorable ruling.

But my law firm, with our lead lawyer Robert Nance at the front, had the guts to stand up to the tobacco companies. Once we decided to take them on, we made the commitment and got busy. The Band of Brothers mobilized. Thirty-seven Riggs Abney lawyers worked on the case. After several tough years, we won.

In 1997, all of the work we and the others had done forced legally mandated concessions and a settlement by the Liggett Group, Inc., one of the world's biggest tobacco companies. The concessions included admissions by Liggett Group representatives that, yes, smoking is addictive and, yes, smoking causes cancer—and oh yes, we do in fact have a marketing strategy to sell cigarettes to minors. This was the fight that got rid of Joe Camel and other cartoon ads that hawked cigarettes and other tobacco products to kids, at least subliminally.

Our law firm got a fee as did the others who worked on the case. We didn't get rich, but we were paid for our years of effort. And the state of Oklahoma received a two *billion* dollar settlement, which has been called the largest settlement in state history. That money has done a lot to help Oklahoma's health care.

It was a worthwhile fight, one of those battles my firm and I have undertaken that help me formulate answers to Martin Luther King's persistent, urgent, and timeless question.

Sarah, dressed as My Fair Lady's Eliza Doolittle, sang Wouldn't It Be Loverly to me at the Lyric Theatre Broadway Ball in 2008. Life does not get any better.

KNOW, LIKE, RESPECT

*You cannot antagonize and persuade at the
same moment.*

When a word like "change" gets thrown around as
much as it was in the presidential campaigns of 2008,
there's always a good reason for it. And when a meeting
of veteran political figures—brought together early
that same year by University of Oklahoma president
David Boren with the stated purpose of encouraging
bipartisan solutions to the nation's challenges—gets
overwhelmingly positive attention in the nation's media
and inspires all sorts of letters and emails to newspaper
editors, it gives a further indication of a new mood
in America.

Will it mark the year that we finally turned the
corner? Will historians see it as the date that a majority
of our people finally got good and fed up with the
paralyzing divisiveness in our political culture?

The jury's still out. But like many, I devoutly hope
that's the case. While I'm waiting to see, I plan to

continue doing my own part to change things on the Oklahoma City–based television show, *Flashpoint*. It's a half-hour political program began in 1992, featuring Burns Hargis and me—with the invaluable aid of our veteran moderator, Kevin Ogle—in which we argued politics and put questions to guests ranging from Pat Robertson and Kenneth Starr to John Kerry and James Carville. Airing 9:30 to 10:00 Sunday mornings on NBC's KFOR Channel 4, *Flashpoint* consistently scores the best ratings of any show in its timeslot.

Now, however, there is no Burns Hargis. He had to leave the show in 2008, after becoming the new president of Oklahoma State University. At the time, we had been together sixteen years, and I'm proud to be able to write that while we disagreed on scores of issues, Republican Hargis and Democrat Turpen nonetheless managed to be civil to one another. As writer Kathryn Jenson White put it in the Spring 2004 issue of *Sooner Magazine*,

> Turpen often interrupts Hargis, and Hargis responds with zingers when he can wrestle the floor from his fast-talking partner. Despite the verbal tumbling, no one gets truly testy.
>
> At a time when most agree the level of American political discourse has sunk so low it has to look up to see down, these two men protect their show and their relationship from the dirt with a three-verb shield.

The verbs that comprise that shield? *Know, like,* and *respect.*

Burns and I know, like, and respect each other, despite the fact that we come from very different places philosophically and politically. The way we tend to explain it is that he's like Descartes—"I think, therefore I am," while I'm more along the lines of Rousseau—"I feel, therefore I am." We are different people with different beliefs, but we have a fundamental respect for each other's point of view.

Also, Burns and I both believe in the axiom that heads this chapter: you cannot antagonize and persuade at the same moment. In *Flashpoint*, we tried to be persuasive instead of antagonistic, which isn't to say that we didn't enjoy zinging the other with a bon mot or two along the way.

The year the show began, Burns and I were both members of Oklahoma City's Rotary Club, so from the start of our television career, when we first sat down in the KFOR studio, we were acquainted and had a mutual respect for one another. But we didn't really become friends until after the show began.

Flashpoint's genesis came when the station hired us both as on-air political analysts for the '92 presidential election. We both say we got the gig because each of us had run for Oklahoma governor and lost. One of my lines is, "Our races for governor were so bad that some say we put the word *goober* in *gubernatorial*." Burns, for his part, has defined a political analyst as a neutered tomcat—close to the action, but only in an advisory capacity.

So the night of the election, he arrived armed with one-liners about Bill Clinton. I had a few of my own concerning Republican George H. W. Bush, and during the course of the evening, we parried and thrust and tried to be amusing at the expense of the other person's candidate. Whatever it was we did, producer Mary Ann Eckstein and news anchor Devin Scillian liked it well enough to offer us a job doing much the same thing every Sunday morning, and her invitation led to a heck of a run.

People tell me that the Descartes-versus-Rousseau analogy is pretty apt, that I came off as a little more emotional on the program, while Burns was more intellectual. Our conversations, in addition, showed that we disagreed about most of the issues raised on the show.

But even though I'm aware this sounds a little presumptuous, both of us really felt as though we were examples for the state legislature, and even for the US Congress, by demonstrating in a weekly television show that political disagreement didn't have to be so vitriolic. We believed you could argue different points of view without despising your opponent, and we tried to make our show an example of that. We didn't vilify each other. We didn't—and don't—hate each other because we disagree. And the implied question asked in every episode of *Flashpoint*—even now—is, Why does it have to be the other way in the state legislature? Why does it have to be that way in Congress?

As the show went along, Burns and I, of course, got to know one another better and better. Our wives are good friends. Our *mothers* are good friends. Burns and I also did banquets and other speaking engagements together all over the state. A few years ago, we were gassing up in Oklahoma City, heading for Mangum for the town's chamber of commerce banquet, and one of our viewers saw us.

"You mean you guys *travel* together?" he asked.

I said, "Well, I drive, and he sits in the backseat reading the *Wall Street Journal* and sipping a glass of champagne."

"Yeah," Burns piped up, "and I wish he'd get that Clinton-Gore sticker off the car."

Part of the shtick is to be forceful enough on Sunday morning with the issues you believe in that people will kind of wonder how good of friends you really are. The truth is that we're two good friends who agreed to disagree. By the time he had to leave the show, we were actually like an old married couple. I could finish his lines, and he could finish mine. It's the darndest thing I've ever seen.

All of this isn't to say that we didn't have to establish some boundaries over the years. The one that jumps out is about our children. My kids go to private schools. His daughter is a Democrat who owns a health-food store in Norman. A couple of times, each of us tried to use one of those facts on the other—until we mutually decided to leave our children out of it.

Frankly, the closest we have gotten to incivility, and maybe even anger at one another, has come with the war in Iraq. He was for the war and wanted to finish it. From the very beginning, I said it was a war searching for a reason. When it started, he wanted to believe the president was right. On the other hand, when George

Bush used the term *shock and awe* early on. I was taken aback by my own country's leader.

So the war is the only thing that kept us a little hot, a little intense with one another after the cameras blinked off. And why not? It's about life and death. He takes it seriously, and so do I.

But even under those circumstances, we could shake hands after the show was over and leave the studio together. That's the magic of the relationship. We can disagree passionately over issues that are very important to Oklahoma, to the United States of America, to the whole world, and still be friends. When he was up for president of OSU, for instance, I was his biggest advocate, and no one was happier than me when he got it.

I'm sometimes asked why we were able to carry on a television show for over a decade and a half, along with lots of public appearances together during that run. Why did *Flashpoint*, and the appearances we made jointly outside the studio, continue to engage people?

I think it's because we brought out the best in each other. And even though our television partnership is over, we still do. He knew when I was getting ready to make a humorous point, and maybe even go for a laugh at his expense—or at least his candidate's expense—and he let me make the point and get the laugh. I knew when he was getting ready to zing my friends Bill and Hillary Clinton, and I let him make *his* point. I might get in a quick counterpunch, but in a debate setting, it's important to have enough patience, enough respect for the other person, that you want him to get

his points in and be as good as he can be. I did that
for him, and he did the same thing for me. It sounds
sort of counterintuitive because any debater wants to
win the debate, and debate is what drives much of
Flashpoint. But as I noted earlier, we both believe you
can't antagonize and persuade in the same moment.

As Burns told *Oklahoma Gazette*'s Brian Brus,
"What we've tried to do is debate civilly. Policy debates
without acrimony will lead to compromise a lot faster."

That was a point our show tried to make every week.
Now with Burns gone to Stillwater, my new *Flashpoint*
partner, Kirk Humphreys, and I are still committed to
remaining civil in all circumstances. I don't have the
history with Kirk, the former Oklahoma City mayor,
that I have with Burns, but Kirk and I continue the style
of discourse that began with the very first broadcast,
moderated by our very own Edward R. Murrow,
Kevin Ogle.

Although I should probably know better, I can only
hope we're beginning to see evidence that the idea of
persuasion over antagonism is spreading throughout
the country and that politicians and political
commentators are finally realizing that civility is not a
sign of weakness, but simply another way of applying
the Golden Rule—giving the same respect you'd like to
get when you express your own opinions.

Every Sunday morning at nine thirty, Kirk and I will
continue to try and be faithful examples of the notion
that you can disagree agreeably—that even if you're
passionately opposed on an issue, it's not necessary, and
may even be counterproductive, to scream or demonize

your opponent simply to make your points. Isn't it time we grew out of that?

SAVE A LIFE

A star shines the brightest when the sky is the darkest.

My friend Ted Richardson was an assistant US attorney in Oklahoma City. More to the point, he was a member of the team that prosecuted Timothy McVeigh in the mid-nineties. Like a lot of us in Oklahoma and elsewhere, he had lost good friends in McVeigh's hideous bombing of the Murrah Federal Building.

Thousands of us who lived and worked in the city then remember exactly what we were doing at 9:02 a.m. on April 19, 1995. Many of us literally heard and felt the explosion that irrevocably changed our lives, our state, and our world. It was left to us to try and do the best we could, with the fears and insecurities that instant of insanity opened up, to try and resume life with our spouses and children, our friends and our faith.

No one emerged from that unscathed. But some weren't able to emerge from it at all.

Ted Richardson, sadly, was one of those people. He lived in my Oklahoma City neighborhood, Crown Heights—which I've long described as a Norman Rockwell painting come to life—and was best friends with my own good friend, Kyle Toal, whom you've met elsewhere in this book. Kyle and I knew that Ted was suffering with something, some deep psychological wounds, and we tried to give him encouragement— thinking that maybe if we gave him *enough* positive reinforcement, it might prove contagious, and his upbeat mental attitude would return.

Sadly, it was not to be. In September of 1997, only a couple of years after the bombing, Ted walked through the park in our neighborhood until he got to a local church in a wooded area. Then outside the building, he took his own life with a shotgun.

When we found out about it, Kyle took it very hard, feeling—as many of us did—that if he'd just tried a little harder or talked to Ted a little more, it wouldn't have happened. Finally, I sat down and said, "Kyle, listen. Ted had an eight-year-old son—other kids as well, but an eight-year-old son. And he had a beautiful wife, Julie. If those things weren't enough to keep him here, what makes you think *you* could have done anything to keep him from doing what he did?"

Ted was loved by many, and he had loved in return. For healthy people, that's often enough for a rich and happy life. But Ted wasn't healthy. He suffered from a disease of the spirit—clinical depression, certainly exacerbated by his nearness to the Oklahoma City bombing and several of its victims. As a September 26, 2001, *Wall Street Journal* article reported,

> In Oklahoma, stress [following the bombing] manifested itself in higher-than-expected divorce rates among fire and police workers, as well as increased incidences of severe depression and drug and alcohol addiction.

A number of other suicides were also linked to that horrendous act and its psychological and spiritual aftermath.

In this era of medical miracles, we expect a treatment or prescription to be able to turn a disease around. But there is no magical medical answer for diseases of the spirit. We tend to think that those who are clinically depressed should be able to heal themselves with enough positive thinking and good thoughts from those around them—but they need much more than that. People who suffer from clinical depression often must undergo years of medical and psychological treatment before they begin to dig themselves out of the dark and hopeless pit they've found themselves in.

Ted's death was a tragedy, very well expressed in our neighborhood newsletter, the *CH-EH* (Crown Heights-Edgemere Heights) *Chronicle*. A piece attributed to "everyone on 39th Street West" ended with this poignant paragraph: "It seems to us like part of the heart and soul of the neighborhood is missing. We are all poorer for the loss of our friend and good neighbor, Ted Richardson."

Ted won't have died in vain if anyone, after reading this chapter, decides to learn more about a family member, friend, or co-worker who suffers from his debilitating disease. I believe we all need to talk as openly about clinical depression as we do about drug and alcohol addiction. And we need to have the courage to intervene in the lives of our loved ones when it becomes clear that positive thinking, love, and prayers aren't going to be enough.

Why this particular chapter title? It's because Ted was a light in my life, and he still is, even though my world—and the worlds of many others—darkened when he died.

I will always depend upon Ted's star, shining like a faraway beacon in the cosmos of my own memory, to provide enlightenment and illumination as I make my way through life, still struggling to understand why he chose to extinguish his own earthly light.

Those who knew Ted Richardson felt their day grow brighter whenever he walked into a room. May his star shine in the souls of those who loved him, lighting up the darkness, showing the way to peace, acceptance, and understanding.

GIVE SECOND CHANCES

Turn setbacks into comebacks.

From my perspective, it was all about doing what I thought was right, about confronting corruption and forcing it out into the open, and the danger that can bring. Ultimately, however, I found it to be about a man who made mistakes, was toppled from power as a result, and laboriously, over years, reestablished himself and his reputation. Given that ending, it could be still another illustration of my belief in the God of second chances.

This chapter begins in the late 1970s, just before then governor David Boren appointed me Muskogee County district attorney. Before I became DA, Julian K. Fite had the job, and I was his assistant. His many accomplishments as DA included leading a grand jury investigation into what *Tulsa Tribune* columnist Jim East called, much later, "a courthouse out of control." In his column in February 28, 1989, East quoted Muskogee attorney A. Camp Bonds on the political environment of the Muskogee courthouse at the time:

"corrupt, contemptible and vicious." Any way you want to describe it, the late seventies amounted to a rough period in the history of Muskogee County.

Julian left to become a US attorney, and I was appointed Muskogee County DA, which made me the prosecutor in the case. So here came Mike Turpen, a carpetbagger from north Tulsa, taking on the corruption in the Muskogee County courthouse like Buford Pusser with his club in the *Walking Tall* movies. And sometimes, things got just about that intense. As the investigation went on and we began pressing for indictments and convictions of judges and others, several of my friends in Tulsa became convinced I was going to be killed. They'd ask me with incredulous voices, "Mike, what are you *doing* over there?"

What I was doing was taking on some of the most powerful people in Muskogee County, and I knew eastern Oklahoma had a long history of people playing for keeps. I'd been accosted, in a roundabout but nonetheless unmistakable way, by an upper-level courthouse employee, who'd made it clear that it'd be a lot easier on everyone—including me, of course—if I'd just back off. I'd be lying if I didn't tell you that I began looking under the hood of my car for a bomb every time I was out of it for any length of time.

But I was Dudley Do-Right; I was on a mission. And every day, after I examined my vehicle's engine for suspicious packages or wiring, I would crank up the ignition and play a cassette of "Sail On," a Grammy-winning song by the gospel group the Imperials. One of the song's lines spoke to me in a major way during those unsettling times: "If the Lord's in control of your life, sail on."

I'd listen to that, and I'd think, "There's a guardian angel watching over you, Mike Turpen, because you're doing what's right. You're cleaning up the courthouse because it's corrupt. You're doing good things. So sail on."

A year or so later, our work had resulted in three convictions and the ouster of a district judge. Among the convicted was an accused judge, who received a five-year prison sentence and a five-hundred-dollar fine for embezzling traffic fines.

"It's tragic, but it's right," I told *Muskogee Daily Phoenix* reporter Nancy Mathis after a jury found the judge guilty. "It's a fair verdict. I think it's an indication that the people of Muskogee don't want corruption in their courthouse."

Although the jury recommended five years in prison, the judge didn't serve any hard time. His lawyers kept up the appeals, and the five-year sentence was ultimately suspended. Five years later, he was disbarred from practicing law.

But that's hardly the end of the story. As East put it in his column,

> He could've run and hid—ashamed to show his face in his native Muskogee. Instead he remained, baling hay in the summer, cutting firewood in the winter, and digging coal and holes for septic tanks to make ends meet.

In the mid-eighties, the former judge also began doing research for the firm of A. Camp Bonds—the Muskogee lawyer who previously described his courthouse in such powerfully negative terms.

In 1989, well over a decade after his conviction, he applied to the Oklahoma Supreme Court to allow him to practice law again.

By that time, I'd been in private practice with Riggs, Abney, Neal, Turpen, Orbison, and Lewis for a couple of years. The former judge hired my friend Larry Derryberry—another former Oklahoma politician—to represent him in his efforts, and Larry called me.

"Would you write a letter to help him get his license to practice law back?" Larry asked. "I know you prosecuted him. I know you convicted him in front of a jury. I know he got five years. I know you believe he was guilty. So what do you think?"

In the years since the conviction, I spoke with many people about the judge, and from the information I put together, I was convinced that he was doing as much as he could to rehabilitate himself. I believed that he was repentant and that he was deserving of a second chance. In my eyes, he had redeemed himself.

So I was more than proud to write a letter for him. Eventually, he was able to practice law again in our state and continues to work as a lawyer today, the head of his own firm in Muskogee.

A few years ago, I saw him standing beside the water cooler in the Muskogee County courthouse. He stuck out his hand and said, "Mike, thanks for writing that letter for me."

When I talked to Jim East back in 1989, during the period the convicted judge was working hard at getting reinstated, I told Jim simply, "It is an impressive comeback."

His setback was an extreme one, and his comeback took years—but today, I still stand by what I told Jim East for his column some twenty years ago. And I was glad that in some small way, I was able to demonstrate my belief in a God of second chances, of forgiveness and redemption, and help turn a particularly tough setback into a dramatic and lasting comeback.

President Bill Clinton and me in a meeting with Oklahoma City bombing victims' family members at the University of Central Oklahoma, hosted by UCO President and former Oklahoma Governor George Nigh, 1997.

LIVE EVERY MINUTE

Do any human beings ever realize life while they live it...every, every minute?

—Thornton Wilder

In *A Man Without a Country*, a sharp and incisive 2005 book comprised of material from his essays and speeches, the great American writer Kurt Vonnegut spent some time remembering his favorite uncle, a man named Alex. Uncle Alex, Vonnegut wrote, not only complained that human beings seldom noticed their own happiness but also did his best to point out happiness where he saw it. So seeing a young Kurt drinking lemonade under an apple tree in the summertime, he would suddenly exclaim, "If this isn't nice, I don't know what is."

My son Patrick has a similar expression for the golden moments we experience as a family. It's at those times that he's likely to proclaim, "This is the life."

Back in September of 2002, I was invited by members of the Georgia Prosecutors Association to

MIKE TURPEN

give an address on trial tactics. The group was meeting at Jekyll Island, a major resort area on the Georgia coast, so I took Patrick along with me, promising him a fishing trip when I was finished with the business end of things.

In a 2003 column, *Dallas Morning News* writer Ray Sasser pondered the reasons that people fish, pointing out that because we're made mostly of water, "There is an inexorable human attraction to the fluid medium. We're drawn to water as undeniably as steel filings are drawn to a magnet."

Certainly, Patrick and I felt a pull toward the beautiful waters that lapped at the island. So we chartered a boat and took off for a likely spot on the Intracoastal Waterway, neither of us knowing it would be the fishing excursion of a lifetime.

After some time on the water, Patrick hooked what turned out to be a 144 1b tarpon—the fish Ernest Hemingway dubbed both the Silver King and "a missile with fins." In what's probably the great American writer's best-known novel, *The Old Man and the Sea*, Hemingway had his fisherman protagonist battle a giant fish for more than two days and nights. Patrick's tarpon adventure didn't last quite that long, but when he was finished, he could relate to the old fisherman's struggles. By the time the guide wrestled the giant fish onto the deck, my son had been fighting it for an incredible three hours! As Patrick, exhausted but exhilarated, watched the Silver King—now referred to in family lore as the Turpen tarpon — being hoisted onto the boat, he turned to me.

"Dad," he said, "this is the life." And indeed it was.

Only a few months later, Susan and I were privileged to take in the Westport County Playhouse production of Thornton Wilder's theatrical classic *Our Town* on Broadway. Featuring Paul Newman as the narrator and familiar television actors Jane Curtin and Frank Converse in the cast, it was a rich and satisfying production of that much-performed evergreen, first produced more than sixty years ago.

One sequence in *Our Town* had a particularly powerful impact on me. It involved young Emily Webb, who dies and then is allowed to look back at one day in her life. She chooses her twelfth birthday, and her agony in realizing the preciousness of everyday living becomes almost unbearable.

"It goes so fast," she shouts, just before breaking down. "We don't have time to look at one another." And then in her tears, she notes that the earth is "too wonderful for anybody to realize," concluding with the statement that begins this chapter.

When I experienced that moment in the theater, I thought back to the memorable day Patrick and I spent on that chartered boat, and I understood how wise Thornton Wilder was. Each of us has so many moments when we can say, like Vonnegut's uncle, "If this isn't nice, I don't know what is," or, like Patrick, simply, "This is the life."

Yet for some reason, we don't say those things—or, at least, we don't say them often enough. Perhaps, as Wilder intimates, in the busyness of living, we simply don't recognize them until it's too late.

I once heard a prayer that began with a request for us to see each new day with joy and wonder. The psalmist wrote that each day was a day God had made, so we should rejoice and be glad in it. Each day, each month, each year does go by in a blink. That's just one of the reasons, I think, why it's important to occasionally take time to look at each other and say, "You know—this is the life."

THINK BIG

If you believe it, you can achieve it.

That little maxim has long been a governing principle in my life. For as long as I can remember, I've believed in dreaming and thinking big and then doing my best to convert those dreams and thoughts into reality.

I started realizing all of that on a conscious level when Oklahoma governor David Boren appointed me district attorney of Muskogee County back in 1977. It was a big break for me, to say the least. I was not from Muskogee. I was a McLain High School grad from north Tulsa. I was called a carpetbagger, an out-of-towner, and a lot worse, I'm sure, by some in Muskogee County. But we got a lot of things accomplished and made a difference in the county and beyond for the five years I held that post.

During that time, my right-hand guy was Drew Edmondson. He'd been a classroom teacher, and then he'd gone to Vietnam. Since he was from a well-known political family in Oklahoma, it was probably inevitable that he'd enter politics, and he did upon his return from the war, winning a state legislative seat. Then he decided to go back to school and get a law degree.

As Muskogee County district attorney, I hired him first as a legal intern and then as assistant DA. We fought a lot of battles together and won quite a few of them.

In 1982, he knew I was thinking about running for attorney general of Oklahoma. And he kind of *wanted* me to run because if I did, he could run for my old job. His dad, the longtime Oklahoma congressman Ed Edmondson, had been Muskogee County DA, and his uncle, J. Howard Edmondson, had been Tulsa County DA before becoming governor. So the family precedent had been set.

I knew Drew would be behind me for other reasons as well. We'd ridden the river together, we'd stayed hitched, and he was someone I knew I could count on. Still, I wasn't entirely sure I wanted to leave the DA's job, where I was making a living and making a difference. If I decided to throw my hat in the ring, I might be up against a powerful opponent in the Democratic primary. Jan Eric Cartwright, the then-current attorney general, had sliced his opponents to ribbons in the previous two primaries and was considered by many observers to be virtually unbeatable.

Word had it, however, that he was going to be running for governor, leaving the field a little more open. So after a lot of deliberation, I decided to give it a shot. And somewhere around that time, Drew gave me a coffee cup illustrated with an oversized pair of cowboy boots and the two-word slogan, "Think BIG!"

So I began crisscrossing the state, appearing before the people every chance I got. I went to political rallies, barbecues, town-hall and main-street meetings, and if there was some get-together I had to miss because of a conflict, I made sure that people involved with my campaign were there to handle questions and hand out my literature.

At first, my opponent appeared content to rest on his laurels, and why not? He was the obvious favorite, and he'd easily taken care of bigger challenges than mine. But by the second week in August, he'd changed his tactics.

"Feisty Turpen Forcing Cartwright to Get Serious," read a headline in *The Sunday Oklahoman* newspaper, published only sixteen days before the August 24 primary elections.

Even for all of that, I was still a definite underdog going into the primaries. But when the votes were counted, I'd come out on top.

"We won, based on organization and involvement, enthusiasm, hard work, and good people," I told *Tahlequah Pictorial Daily Press* writer Barbara Bashore in September, a couple of weeks after the August primary elections. "I don't know how many people told me, 'You can't win, but I'll vote for you.' I'd tell them, 'That's all I want—your vote.' And we pulled it off.

"For me," I added, referring to the win, "it is pretty much a dream come true. I've been on a political roll ever since high school, and I learned back then you can't win alone. People have to be working *with* you, not just *for* you."

Of course, Drew Edmondson was one of those people. And even he probably doesn't really know what a motivator that coffee cup was. For one thing, it fit well with one of my campaign slogans of the time, which was, "Mike Turpen—Tough as a Boot." My calling cards even had little boots on them.

But it was much more than that. Every day I came to work, I looked at that coffee cup. And to me, the corollary to "Think BIG!" was, "If you believe it, you can achieve it." In other words, the whole key was to think big, believe in what you're thinking, and then go out and achieve it.

More than a quarter of a century later, I still have that cup—and that philosophy. And to this good day, when I've got a big decision to make, I'll look at Drew's gift for inspiration.

Think BIG! Do that, and you can find yourself doing some exciting, and even unusual, things—starring in an independent movie, for instance.

My friends Butch and Ben McCain were mainstays of Oklahoma City television for many years. Now working on the West Coast, they are singer-songwriters as well as filmmakers, and I've been lucky enough to be involved with them in both pursuits. I contributed lyrics and got co-writing credit on two songs they recorded, "Faith, Family and Friends" and "Share the Joy," and I got to act in their comedy-horror feature, *Killer Tumbleweeds*, which started gaining a little national momentum following its spring 2009 screening at

Oklahoma City's Lyric Theatre, the 1935 movie theater I raised ten million dollars to save. I play a senator in the picture, and my kids Patrick and Sarah cameo as tumbleweed-attack survivors. It's a truly funny picture.

I enjoy getting laughs from audiences. I make a point to include as much humor as the situation warrants when I speak to a group. It seems to work. After a July 2009 speech in Colorado, Attorney General John Suthers had this to say in a letter to me:

> All the reviews are in and you're the biggest hit on the Colorado Attorney General's office stage in at least 100 years. Many people wanted to know why you don't make regular comedic appearances on Letterman or Conan O'Brien.

Closer to home, there's our long-running local TV show, *Flashpoint*, which continues to draw good ratings. I also recently became an investor in the Broadway musical *Memphis*, the story of the birth of rock 'n' roll, which opened at the Shubert Theatre in fall of '09.

These days, in my middle age, my deliberations about whether or not to take on a new project have more to do with time than anything else. As you get older, you get more aware of "Time's winged chariot hurrying near," as the poet Andrew Marvell eloquently put it, and I always have to ask myself if a potential new endeavor is something I should commit a big chunk of my time and energy to. Is it something I believe is necessary, and worthwhile, and contributing to the common good? Or as in the case of movies, music, and

Broadway involvement, is it something that could be a lot of fun?

Since leaving the political arena for private practice as an attorney, much of my effort has gone toward various kinds of fundraising, whether in the form of capital campaigns or coming up with money for candidates and causes I believe in, whether it's Hillary Clinton or the Lyric Theatre.

I'm sure Drew didn't know my world would end up, in some ways, revolving around that little coffee cup. Its slogan, "Think BIG!" took me to the Oklahoma AG's office. It took me to Broadway and the silver screen. And it's taken me to a lot of places in-between.

My Mom, Marge, once told Frosty, Brent, and me, "Put your signature on this planet." I continue to be challenged by her motivational admonition, making new trysts with life---ES, EM, ED. Indeed tomorrow is another day, a gift. It comes in at midnight with a clean slate--a blank tablet, as John Locke would suggest. Recognizing that the years are short, but the days are long, we must seize full advantage of every moment God provides us.

Sandra Day O'Connor tells us that the secret to happiness is essentially wrapped up in three words: WORK THAT MATTERS. We must pursue our passion with unflinching determination and in so doing be guided by the eloquent verse of the 18th Century poet William Blake:

"To see the World in a grain of sand
And Heaven in a Wild Flower,
Hold Infinity in the Palm of your hand
And Eternity in an Hour."

ACKNOWLEDGMENT

If you asked me if I could write a book about my life and how I have lived it, about my experiences, my friends, my family, and parenthood, I would have to reply that I could not write such a book, at least not without a lot of help. And in this effort, I have had a lot of help. My lovely wife, Susan, and my three wonderful children, Sean, Patrick, and Sarah, all contributed in more ways than I can describe to every page of this book. My mom Marge, Bob, and my brothers, Brent and Frosty, inspired me, and their contributions are woven into these pages throughout. My friend Bill Bernhardt, the famous Oklahoma author, provided much encouragement and help in organizing my ideas. He also introduced me to John Wooley, who was immensely helpful in putting it all together. If you want to write a book, call John. He is a master at helping you organize your random thoughts, legal-pad outlines, yellowed newspaper articles, and old videotapes into a meaningful manuscript. His creative genius is alive and well on every page of this book.

Hillary Clinton, George Kaiser, Deana McCloud and me at the Woody Guthrie Center enjoying the display of the original lyrics of "This Land Is Your Land." Clinton was in Tulsa to recognize the George Kaiser Family Foundation for their commitment to early childhood education, 2014.

ABOUT THE AUTHOR

Michael C. Turpen was born in Tulsa, Oklahoma, educated in Tulsa Public Schools, and graduated from the University of Tulsa earning a bachelor of science degree in history and a juris doctor degree. In 1982, Mr. Turpen was elected attorney general for the state of Oklahoma. He served as Muskogee County district attorney from 1977 to 1982. Since 1987, Mr. Turpen has been a partner in the law firm of Riggs, Abney, Neal, Turpen, Orbison & Lewis in Oklahoma City, Oklahoma.

While no longer serving in public office, Mr. Turpen remains politically active. He appears weekly on Oklahoma City NBC-affiliate KFOR's award-winning public-affairs show, *Flashpoint with Turpen & Humphreys*. He appeared twice on ABC's *Politically Incorrect* with Bill Maher and was featured on PBS' national documentary, *Vote for Me: Politics in America*. He had a long-running monthly column, Turpen Time, for the OPEA monthly newspaper and was a featured columnist for Microsoft's internet magazine,

Slate. Mr. Turpen is a nationally sought-after public speaker, having keynoted conferences of the National Association of Attorneys General, the Fourth Federal Judicial Circuit, and the National Family and Juvenile Judges Association.

Mr. Turpen has received numerous awards, honors, and appointments. In 2010, Mike was inducted into the Oklahoma Hall of Fame, the state's highest honor. In 2008, Mike received the Oklahoma Arts Council Governor's Award for Community Service; Treasures for Tomorrow Award from the Oklahoma Health Center Foundation; and the Urban Pioneer Award from the Plaza District Association. In 2007, Mike received the Oklahoma Bar Association's William Paul Distinguished Service Award; recognition from the Clinton Global Initiative for his work with Burns Hargis for Legal Aid of Oklahoma; the Outstanding Volunteer Fundraiser Award from the Association of Fundraising Professionals, Oklahoma Chapter; and the John F. Kennedy Award for Community Service, given by the Oklahoma City Knights of Columbus.

In 2006, Mike received the John Kirkpatrick Award from Lyric Theatre for his leadership in chairing their successful $10 million capital campaign. In 2004, the courtroom at the University of Tulsa College of Law was named the Price-Turpen Courtroom to honor Mike's service to his alma mater. In 2004, Mike also received the National Association of Attorneys General Francis X. Bellotti Award for outstanding service to the association. In 2003, Mike served as honorary chairman of the Urban League of Oklahoma City. In 2002, he established the Melvin C. Hall Leadership Scholarship at Langston University. In 2000, he was named Outstanding Alumnus for the University of Tulsa.

He was appointed by President Bill Clinton to the President's Advisory Council on the Arts at the Kennedy Center in 1992. In 1986, Mike was the recipient of the National Foundation for the Improvement of Justice Award and was honored by the National Organization for Victim Assistance as one of Ten Outstanding National Leaders in the field of victim rights over the past decade. Mr. Turpen was listed in *Esquire Magazine*'s 1985 register, "Men and Women under 40 Who are Changing the Nation." In 1980, he was the winner of the Oklahoma Bar Association's Maurice Merrill Golden Quill Award for outstanding contributions to the *Oklahoma Bar Journal*. In 1979, Mr. Turpen was named Outstanding Young Man by the Muskogee Jaycees and Outstanding Young Oklahoman by the Oklahoma Jaycees. In 1975, he was selected by the Oklahoma Bar Association as Oklahoma's Outstanding Young Lawyer.

Mike's interests are many and varied. He is president of the Lyric Theatre Board of Directors and on the boards of the Oklahoma City National Memorial and Museum, Oklahoma State Fair Board, Oklahoma State Regents for Higher Education and Allied Arts. He a member of the Oklahoma Academy of State Goals, Rotary Club, Oklahoma Business Roundtable, the Economic Club of Oklahoma, Advisory Board for the University of Tulsa College of Law, and the Creativity

Project. Mike has served as president and board member of the CARE Center, Oklahoma City.

He is the founder of the Young Men's Poetry Club. Mike argued before the United States Supreme Court in 1985. He served as president of the Oklahoma District Attorneys Association, vice president of the National Organization of Victim Assistance (NOVA), and vice chairman of Oklahoma's Crime Commission. Mr. Turpen is a member of the American, Oklahoma, Tulsa County, and Oklahoma County Bar Associations, as well as being a founding fellow of the Oklahoma Bar Foundation and a faculty member of the National College of District Attorneys.

Mr. Turpen is married to wife, Susan, and has three children, Sean, Patrick and Sarah. He is a member of Westminster Presbyterian Church in Oklahoma City where he is currently active as a teacher for the confirmation class and on the WPC Foundation Board of Directors.

"I EXIST TO ASSIST."